What Others Are Saying About

Confessions of a Hiring Manager

"J.T. Kirk has written the ultimate guide for properly positioning yourself for a job offer in this or any economy. No question is left unanswered in the process and the job seeker receives valuable and powerful perspective from a hiring manager. From cover letter to compensation negotiations and from résumé structure to interviewing strategy, this book covers it all. This is a comprehensive guide for professionals interested in paving the path to an offer."

LaDonna Wernli, CFE, PHR
Human Resource Manager
Association of Certified Fraud Examiners

"The information in this book gives job seekers a distinctly competitive edge, especially in today's job market. I highly recommend it!"

Brian Jud
Author of Job Search 101, Coping With Unemployment, and The Art of Interviewing

"*Confessions of a Hiring Manager* offers job seekers advice on getting the hiring manager's attention and provides great insight for hiring managers to ensure the best candidate gets the job. Although written primarily for job seekers and career changers, the excellent perspective from J.T. Kirk will help hiring managers and HR personnel improve their hiring process—from job posting to final offer. Readers should also take advantage of the many free online assessments on J.T. Kirk's website."

Kate Katlin
Kate Katlin Associates Executive Recruiters

Confessions of a Hiring Manager is not just another book on getting a job: the market already is saturated with such books by business writers, résumé writers, and career coaches with advice on how to write an attention-grabbing cover letter and résumé, or how to "ace" the interview.

While the efforts of such professionals may provide some help and value, it is the **hiring manager** who ultimately determines who gets hired. The hiring manager's perspective offers valuable insight into unwritten corporate hiring practices and guidance on how to address an organization's needs. Résumé writers or career coaches offer a perspective of being on the outside looking in; the hiring manager is already on the inside and knows the subtleties that give one candidate the edge over others who may be equally qualified.

Veteran hiring manager J.T. Kirk provides insight into those qualities hiring managers need and want in addition to the requisite skills, experience, and knowledge prospective candidates offer. Kirk shows job seekers and career changers—including military veterans returning to the civilian workforce—how to package their work history into a Professional Skills, Knowledge, and Experience Portfolio (*PSKE Portfolio™*) that separates the value-add candidate from all other applicants. In addition, he shares strategies for negotiating the best possible compensation package without leaving money on the table.

Confessions of a Hiring Manager offers a view from the other side of the desk that reveals the perspectives, presuppositions, and expectations hiring managers have of people looking for a job or a new career.

While résumé writers and career coaches may give you a fish to feed you for a day, *Confessions of a Hiring Manager* teaches you how to fish so you can feed yourself for a lifetime.

Kings Crown Publishing

Confessions

of a
Hiring Manager

Sage Advice for Fearless
Job Seekers and
Career Changers
in a Confused Economy

CONFESSIONS OF A HIRING MANAGER: SAGE ADVICE FOR
FEARLESS JOB SEEKERS AND CAREER CHANGERS IN A
CONFUSED ECONOMY

Library of Congress Cataloging-in-Publication Data

Kirk, J.T., 1951 –
    Confessions of a hiring manager: sage advice for fearless job seekers
    and career changers in a confused economy/J.T. Kirk
    -1ª ed. First Printing (March 2010)

    LCCN: 2009935283
    ISBN-13: 978-0-9814857-1-3
    ISBN-10: 0-9814857-1-5

VOLUME DISCOUNTS AVAILABLE FOR CORPORATIONS,
ASSOCIATIONS, AND ORGANIZATIONS
For more information, contact the publisher.

PRINTED IN THE UNITED STATES OF AMERICA

Confessions
of a
Hiring Manager

Sage Advice for Fearless
Job Seekers and
Career Changers
in a Confused Economy

J.T. Kirk

KINGS
CROWN
PUBLISHING

Acknowledgements

THE IDEA FOR THIS BOOK germinated from an article I wrote a few years ago for an issue of a professional society monthly journal. The interest in the article later became the impetus for half-day workshops I presented at local meetings, then regional conferences for professional societies. Eventually, it became a one-day workshop that was offered to a variety of national audiences.

Appreciation goes out to all the people who attended the half-day and full-day workshops and who have encouraged me to share this knowledge with others in book form. To those good folks: your success in landing the jobs you wanted or with changing careers using the techniques and skills outlined in this book is testament to their effectiveness. And thanks to Kings Crown Publishing who saw value in the content.

There are no magic bullets or secret formulas for finding a job or changing careers in a good or bad economy, especially with so many variables beyond your control. You have to work and rework your strategy, with an understanding of what hiring managers need. In the job market, sometimes all the rules are not so obvious, particularly those that hiring managers use to screen job candidates for available positions. More often than not, however, it is the candidate who breaks the rules in this highly competitive job market who gets noticed. Those who follow no strategy at all pay a heavy price for their folly, particularly when unemployment benefits run their course and people must take drastic measures to survive.

Whether you are changing jobs or careers, or simply trying to find another job after losing one, it is my hope that you use this information to navigate successfully through the treacherous landscape of the current job market, and to propel your career into a rewarding livelihood and vocation.

Dedication

This book is dedicated to the thousands upon thousands of people of all ages, skills, professions, and education levels who are between jobs; to the breadwinners who have cried a river over the frustration of not finding work or meaningful careers; who have gone through savings accounts, "mattress money," investments, heirlooms, and homes in the process; to those who earnestly await the postman each day, with the hope of receiving just one positive response from the hundreds of job applications or résumés you have mailed—I lived that kind of angst and suffering once many years ago.

J. T. Kirk

About the Author

J.T. KIRK HAS BEEN A hiring manager in both technical and marketing capacities for the energy industry, government research arena, and high-tech sector. Besides providing personal assistance to individuals changing jobs and careers, Kirk also writes books on job and career strategies.

J.T. Kirk resides in Texas with his wife, but dreams about retiring in the Tuscan hills of San Gimignano.

Special Dedication

To my wonderful father and my greatest hero, Donald...

October 28, 1924 – March 30, 2009

...and to my loving mother, Shirley, who courageously endures each day without him.

Table of Contents

Preface

THROUGHOUT MY 20-YEAR CAREER as a hiring manager in different fields, I have seen one qualified candidate after another fail to get hired for a job vacancy because they simply did not understand whose needs they were trying to fulfill. They did not know how to position and sell themselves in their cover letters and résumés as the problem solvers I needed. It was frustrating to see so many people snatching defeat from the jaws of victory.

As a hiring manager in the energy and technology sectors, I gauged the cover letters, résumés, and interview techniques of job candidates based on the methods and strategies in this book, and the majority of the time, their efforts fell short of being successful. They treated the entire job-change or career-change process as a desperate plea for work (and in many instances it is—you just can not let that become the driving force) instead of the strategic operation it is, complete with specific tactics designed to position themselves as the ideal candidates, and to finish with receipt of a great job offer.

The idea of being a confident self-promoting candidate works best when you have the skills, experience, and knowledge as a foundation. Today's job-interview environment demands preparation, practice, and a bit of panache to be successful. Given two or more candidates with equal skills and abilities, the one that best addresses the issues and concerns of the hiring manager will more often than not be the choice for the available position.

I have used the methods in this book to help many friends, family members, and co-workers repackage their professional expertise through what I call the *Professional Skills, Knowledge, and Experience Portfolio (PSKE Portfolio™)*, which is simply a way of presenting your documented "personal intellectual property" in a manner that hiring managers will remember.

I have also helped many others through national workshops and training sessions secure new jobs or careers in less time than they could have on their own through these *PSKE Portfolios*. These chapters detail the methods that have served me and many others well through job changes within industries or career changes altogether. Applicants who understand the many other priorities competing for a hiring manager's attention in addition to how hiring managers approach filling vacant positions will be at a distinct advantage over others just hoping for the best.

While I continue to help people all over the country mostly through one-on-one personal consultation sessions to design their *PSKE Portfolios*, coach them in interview techniques and compensation negotiation, the best way to get this information disseminated to as many people who wanted it was to put it in a book. I have assembled many of the strategies I offer to individual clients into the pages of *Confessions of a Hiring Manager.* This book will show many more job seekers and career changers how to:

- Plan a job-search strategy that confidently and assertively fulfills the needs of *others* first instead of the desperate, ill-thought-out attempt to try to fill *yours* (you will learn why this is important)

- Design your own *PSKE Portfolio* to promote your intellectual property assets to potential employers

- Get an interview based on your *cover letter* alone

- Grab a résumé screener or hiring manager's attention within the first seven seconds of reading a cover letter

- Avoid entries on your résumé that squash any hope of being called in for an interview

- Include entries on your résumé that demand you be brought in for an interview

- Craft an interview-demanding *reverse chronological* résumé if you want to remain in the same field but want to change employers

- Craft an interview-demanding *functional* résumé if you want to move out of one field and into another or if you are a college graduate with no experience

- Create more than one version of your skill set on your résumé (shame on you if you have only one version of your résumé)
- Show returning veterans how to translate military job skills into functional areas of expertise in demand in the civilian job market
- Leave potential employers with the most favorable impression of all candidates after your interview
- Continue to sell yourself long after the interview
- Negotiate the highest possible compensation package *without fear*

Rather than include countless examples of good and bad cover letters and good and bad résumés in this book, I have included in *Appendix A: Resources* some tips and suggestions for exploring what other advice is available for free—including websites that provide job information for veterans, the best paying contracting positions (when that permanent full-time position is illusive), and how to find the "Top 10" of anything job-related on the Internet (lists printed in books get stale fast).

The few cover letter and résumé examples in the book are drawn from actual job applicants (the names on these documents as well as the names of people in the actual stories throughout this book have been changed to protect the clueless and the brilliant) so you can see a representative sample of what to do and what not to do to get the attention of the hiring manager. Getting noticed is as much about the confident attitude conveyed in cover letters as it is the actual documented skills, knowledge, and experience on the résumé.

Regardless of the state of the economy, there will always be demand for highly skilled workers because employers understand that much of what makes these folks skilled is not limited to one job, one trade, one profession, or one industry. Highly skilled and knowledgeable workers have valuable intellectual property that transfers within and across many industries. That is something no one can take away from you whether you want to change jobs, look for a new career, or have to get back into the job market after a layoff, a divorce, or after sending the youngest off to college. You have what employers want and need; it is simply a matter of connecting to the right companies with that need, addressing the concerns of the hiring manager, and positioning yourself as the best available problem solver.

To be sure, changing or finding a new job or career in this economy is going to be challenging to say the least, and it may take you longer than you expect to land a decent-paying job— and very possibly one that is not in your specific field or even first choice. But once you are working at *any* job—even part time—it is always easier to find another job when you already have one (you will read that more than once in this book). If you are not yet working, take heart; for the techniques and tactics described in this book will help you get back on track in the shortest time possible and with better odds of landing a job.

The information in this book is also the result of more than 20 years experience not only helping my employers find the most qualified candidates for open positions, but helping the most qualified candidates find the jobs and careers they wanted. The most rewarding part of it all is seeing people build successful professional lives with just a little guidance and counsel here, maybe a bit of advice and encouragement there—and OK, maybe some nudging from time to time.

You will not find any revolutionary approaches for creating cover letters or résumés, or guarantees for getting hired. What you will find are suggestions, tips, and techniques from a hiring manager's perspective on how to get the attention of other hiring managers with job vacancies to fill. I will share with you the strategies and tactics I have taught others for positioning themselves as the best possible candidate for job vacancies.

And finally, I believe the subtitle of the book captures the essence of the successful job seeker or career changer—*fearless* in the face of increased competition for fewer open positions; *daring* in the midst of a confused economy; *courageous* despite the weight of discouragement, and ultimately, *determined* to overcome it all.

Coping with the stress of prolonged unemployment affects every family member of the unemployed. Coping is a catch-all term for cognitive strategies we all use to relieve stress, and we do that by managing our reactions to a situation rather than trying to alter *all* facets of the stressful circumstance.

In fact, our approach should be one that embraces this coping strategy: "God grant me the serenity to accept the things I cannot change, the courage to change the things I can, and the wisdom to know the difference.

Let me refer the reader to www.jtkirk-author.com where there are a variety of free assessments and tip sheets available to help you evaluate the strength of your cover letter through your salary negotiation strategy, and everything in between.

Let's get started.

Chapter 1
Oops: 2008 – 2009 Happens (and maybe 2010, too)

HAVE YOU HEARD? THE RECESSION IS OVER! According to many economists citing economic indicators, on or about September 15th, the nation's economy emerged from the worst recession since the Great Depression nearly 80 years ago. But we still have a problem: People continue to lose their jobs each month.

There is no doubt that the current economy and employment environment forces you to adapt your thinking to new creative levels to the conditions in the job market. Let's briefly survey the surrounding economic landscape before plotting a course through it.

Unemployment has reached 10.2 percent in October 2009 and the employment outlook for 2010 is dimming as well. The big jobless increase in October signaled weakness in the small business sector—where the nation's job health is often measured. Businesses with fewer than 20 employees account for 25 percent of all jobs but generate 40 percent of job growth in the last recovery, according to the Small Business

1

Administration. These job "nurseries" have to contend with tight credit markets, limited exports (small businesses are less likely to export products and therefore can not benefit from blossoming economies overseas), and rising health-care costs that tend to climb faster than for large companies.

The same economists and market watchers are also claiming that while the economy has emerged from the recession, the recovery will very likely be one that does not include a substantial jobs recovery—at least those same types of jobs will not be replaced with identical vacancies when employers begin hiring again in larger numbers later in 2010 (at the earliest). That presents a unique challenge for many in and out of the job market today.

Employment projections from government and private publications are always a mix of good news/bad news, depending on which industry you happen to be working in at the time and where you are geographically. The average worker today changes careers seven times for a variety of reasons, and more people than ever before are doing so. Retirement used to mean getting out of the rat race altogether and just enjoying the grandkids, golfing, fishing, traveling, and napping. Retirement for many people meant launching a business or a new career altogether out of a preference (or need) to do something different. Whichever definition of retirement you prefer, I think we would all like to be doing it sooner than later—but then...oops.

2008 happened and bled into 2009, which will spill over to 2010. Lehman Brothers, AIG, Bernie Madoff, unaccountable government bailouts of Wall Street and the auto industry, subprime mortgages, collateralized mortgage-backed securities, mortgage derivatives, and other greed-inspired fraud schemes caused a near collapse of the world economy. Money stopped flowing from consumers as people cut back on purchases; banks tightened credit for consumers and businesses; businesses had to rely on cash reserves to continue operation. Eventually, as cash reserves dwindled, more drastic cost-reduction practices had to be put into effect: the downsizing of the American workforce to the tune of over 10 percent, though some estimates place the "true" unemployment numbers much higher. Unemployment numbers are in fact higher for minorities, teenagers, high-school graduates, and high-school dropouts.

Now, retirement for many workers has been postponed indefinitely as retirement funds have dwindled or disappeared altogether, and obtaining a line of credit to start or expand a business is more difficult if not near impossible.

None of this is news if you have been reading the newspaper, watching TV, or surfing the news sites on the Internet, but it does help put an honest perspective on the job market, and perhaps present a clearer picture of what viable options are still available.

The Confused Economy

Economists like to use a variety of indicators as measures of economic health. Based on marginally positive news from the sale of autos and homes as well as the gross domestic product, most economists polled in the *Blue Chip Economic Indicators* publication believe the recession "turned the corner" at the end of September. For July 2009, the dip in the unemployment rate went from 9.5 percent to 9.4 percent—positive news, for sure—but the October unemployment rate topped out at 10.2 percent, while the stock market flew past the 10,000 mark. A confused economy, indeed.

The full impact of the $800 billion stimulus package will not be apparent for quite some time, especially considering that only 10 percent of it has ever been spent as of October 2009. Even as the number of jobless workers soared to nearly 15 million nationwide in September 2009, some 2.6 million jobs remained open, according to the U.S. Department of Labor. Nearly 7 million jobs have disappeared since the recession began in December 2007, and it would be simplistic to think that an economic recovery would include bringing back most of those same jobs. To be sure, the "new" economy will create new jobs but many of them will be different from the mix that was present prior to this most recent economic recession.

Many companies across a variety of industries have learned to be more efficient with fewer employees in operations, manufacturing, distribution, marketing and sales. Many are reluctant to staff up too soon, preferring instead to wait until the economy shows more consistent stability over more than one or two quarters.

The Outlook for Hiring

A March 2009 survey (*Managing Talent in a Turbulent Economy*) of 400 large companies by accounting giant Deloitte concluded that employees with critical skills and in key positions are now at risk of being laid off as repercussions of the down economy continue to radiate through businesses. Forty-three percent of those executives surveyed stated that "role necessity" determined which employees would be next in line for layoffs. In addition, job security could no longer be tied to past and current job performance according to 45 percent of managers surveyed.

So here we are. The workplace environment has never been as stressful as it has been recently as those who have survived rounds of layoffs have to take up the slack left behind by those no longer around, wondering if the other shoe will drop on them in the meantime. For those still fortunate enough to be employed, nearly one-third can expect lower compensation and reduced benefits, and almost 40 percent can plan on the elimination of discretionary perks such as subsidized health club dues, parking, valet services, and food subsidies, according to the Deloitte survey.

While contractor workers, part-time workers, offshore workers, and "fresh-out" workers (recent college graduates) would see a decline in hiring over the next 12 months, the one bright spot in the Deloitte survey indicated experienced, skilled workers would still have some demand in the marketplace. Twenty-seven percent of companies in the survey expected to increase the hiring of experienced employees.

A fresh crop of college graduates has to decide whether to take a chance in the job market now, or go back to school to get an advanced degree. People with college degrees have the lowest unemployment rate (4.5 percent), while those with just a high-school (or less) education have the highest.

Looking Forward

Starting a career out of school, changing companies in mid-career—or changing careers altogether has never been more competitive, more aggravating, and more stressful. Job or career change is not just about your skills, knowledge, and experience—it also includes how you package all that in a manner that best represents not only your past accomplishments but your ability to deliver and achieve great things in the future wherever you are headed.

Regardless of your current career or job situation, you should know what the future projections look like for that field of interest so you can plan accordingly. The most comprehensive set of employment statistics is managed by the

U.S. Bureau of Labor Statistics, which is a branch of the Department of Labor. You can download for free the latest employment projections and employment statistics (see *Appendix A: Resources* for more information).

I do not want to belabor the point. While the jobs picture is bleak, there are in fact companies in many industries that are hiring (health care, government, energy, education, professional/business services, and leisure/hospitality) though the competition for available positions will be intense. However, there are alternatives that can help sustain you as you continue your job or career search (be sure to read *Chapter 9: Other Options: Temp Work, Independent Contracting, and Working for Free*).

Being a fearless job seeker or career changer means you understand the risks, challenges, and obstacles that confront you in your daily efforts to find a job, change jobs, or change careers altogether. There is power and strength in knowing what you are up against because that knowledge empowers you; it forces you to consider more creative ways of getting the job or career you want; it can even transform you into a more confident, assertive, and assured self-promoter that can make you the candidate of choice with hiring managers.

Thinking outside the box can and does get the attention of hiring managers.

A Little Creativity Won't Hurt Your Efforts

My cousin Sheri lost her job in the finance department of a high-tech company based in New England. I helped her create a Professional Skills, Knowledge, and Experience Portfolio *(PSKE Portfolio™)* and a few months later, she was on the short list for a vacant slot in the finance department at a major corporation that packaged and sold seafood around the world. Prior to being called for a second interview, Sheri learned from the hiring manager's executive assistant what his favorite cookies were. She showed up for her second interview with a batch of fresh-baked cookies—and got hired.

Bribery? Some may see it that way but the cookies were offered to others in the office—the cookies just happened to be the hiring manager's favorite kind. What a creative coincidence. Was it the cookies that got her hired? Hardly. It was, after all, her second interview; the cookies simply reinforced her name and her *PSKE Portfolio* with the hiring manager.

My friend Eric found himself in a similar situation. He asked me for any last-minute suggestions (other than baking cookies) just before his interview. I suggested he pay attention to the personal items displayed on the hiring manager's desk or wall. They often provide clues to the things that are important outside of the hiring manager's work environment, and may help establish some rapport with the hiring manager beyond the normal small talk preceding the harder interview questions.

We all want to work with people we like, and that includes hiring managers.

Eric later told me that the hiring manager was a Houston Astros baseball fan and Eric (a New York Yankees fan) was able to engage him in some banter about a subject they both had an interest in. After Eric's very positive interview, he purchased two tickets (less than $30) to a Round Rock Express baseball game (the Express is the local farm team for the Houston Astros) and dropped them off at the hiring manager's office. Eric mentioned to the hiring manager that he would not be able to attend the game, so he thought the hiring manager would know someone who might be interested in using the tickets. Eric purchased the tickets *after* his initial interview as a creative way for the hiring manager to remember him from among the other candidates.

Bribery? Not really because the tickets made their way into someone else's hands (Eric knew the hiring manager could not accept the gift), so there was no intentional or perceived *quid pro quo* from such a transaction—other than the hiring manager remembering Eric's positive interview and, of course, the gesture with the baseball game tickets.

Eric's strategy of doing something different to be remembered paid off. He did receive a job offer from this company, but he turned it down for a more rewarding out-of-state position.

To be clear: these two examples of creativity were not cheap tricks. Neither of these examples would have been successful if both Sheri and Eric did not already have strong cover letters, résumés, and interviews. They simply used cookies and baseball tickets as outside-the-box tactics in their overall strategy to keep their names and their qualifications at the front of the line, assuming all other factors being equal among remaining qualified candidates.

A Final Word

The economic and employment factors that exert an influence on both the job market and corporate hiring practices fluctuate on a frequent basis. But understand this: regardless of the state of the economy, the hiring manager is always pressured to do more with less. In the good times, that means the workload usually increases faster than the headcount does; in a tough economic climate, it often means the workload increases because there are fewer members on the team to do the work.

If you understand the hiring manager's dilemma and can speak to that quandary with a *PSKE Portfolio* that is second to none, believe me—many a hiring manager will take his or her case to executive management to obtain a requisition to hire you—even in the face of a hiring freeze. I have done it and so have many of my peers.

It is easy to become discouraged if you listen to politicians on both sides of the aisle in Congress, political pundits, and cable news talking heads argue the same set of statistical number but with different interpretations about what those numbers reveal on the economy, jobs, health care, etc. Mark Twain once wrote in the *Des Moines Register*: "Get your facts first; then you can distort them how you please." Surround yourself by a wall of immunity to the *emotional effects* of such numbers and opinions, but do remain aware of the economic and employment landscape so you can adjust your strategy and tactics accordingly.

Stay focused, prepare in earnest, and follow the suggestions and techniques outlined in this book and you will improve your odds of (1) being noticed by hiring managers, (2) getting invitations for interviews, and (3) reducing the time between job or career changes. Fearless job seekers or career changers are in command of how they will apply their intellectual resources and creativity to seek out promising jobs or careers regardless of the state of the economy, the statistics, or the influence of things beyond their control.

Now that you have an idea of what you are up against, it is time to devise a strategy that will help you overcome the obstacles that are in *your* control on your way to a job or new career.

11

Chapter 2
Why You Need to Get the Attention of the Hiring Manager

YOU PROBABLY WILL NEVER RECEIVE a business card with "hiring manager" listed as someone's job title. A "hiring manager" is more of a functional role than a job title; many managers of other people find themselves involved with that role from time to time when the manager's team has requisitions for adding to headcount. Some managers do not have any hiring authority—it all depends on how the company structures management duties and responsibilities.

As a manager with hiring responsibilities, my workload was often at maximum capacity. Hiring managers sometimes sidestep those tasks that distract, interfere, or impede the completion of the very objectives on which we and our teams are evaluated each year by upper management. When we successfully complete assigned projects that generate revenue for the company, we keep our jobs. Very simple process.

The two biggest intrusions into my day were meetings and the hiring process. Both have their relative importance in the

13

grand scheme of the corporate environment, but by and large, the attention they demanded often coincided with critical project schedules. Whenever I could, I avoided non-critical meetings; however, résumé screening and interviewing were tasks that required my time and attention, regardless of the project workload or schedules.

I once participated on a panel discussion with other hiring managers at a national conference. During the audience question-and-answer session, someone asked, "How do you approach the résumé evaluation process?" I replied that in my experience, the résumé evaluation process is a necessary intrusion into more important project priorities, and that reading résumés and cover letters, for me, was a bit of a chore because the majority of them were so poorly written and did a terrible job understanding and responding to the business need. I added that any hiring manager who said otherwise was either not busy enough or was not providing "full disclosure."

The hiring manager sitting next to me said, "Well, I enjoy reading cover letters and résumés. It makes my day more interesting." Six months later, I learned she lost her job because project schedules for which she was responsible kept slipping.

At least she had some interesting reading for awhile.

Starting the Hiring Process

The hiring process begins with a need. Each company has its own specific process but basically, a department or project team realizes that there is more work than people to do the work, and discussions begin for how many positions are needed. Such discussions may include an assessment of how much revenue might be gained by hiring others; or perhaps, how much revenue might be lost if no hiring occurs. Both options require an ability to project future needs based on current activities.

For many hiring managers, the decision to hire additional staff is a cautious one, because no hiring manager wants a team to be "fat" (too many people, not enough work). Such a situation can reflect negatively on a hiring manager's ability to predict future project workloads and result in layoffs.

Once a justification for increasing headcount is documented, the case usually is taken to upper management, and with their approval, forwarded on to HR to alert them to begin their respective process (placing ads in various media, contacting headhunters for résumés, etc.).

Why (Many) Hiring Managers Don't Enjoy Screening Résumés

The majority of résumés and cover letters I received for the various positions for which my employers were interviewing often only feebly addressed the requirements for the advertised position. I lost count of the number of cover letters that began: "To Whom It May Concern: Please find enclosed my résumé for the position as advertised..." (if even a résumé was accompanied by a cover letter) or résumés that began with the totally useless, self-serving "Objectives" section, or were structured in a way that forced me to embark on a fishing expedition for the information I needed. Was anyone aware of the seven-second rule about getting someone's attention? My hiring manager peers agreed, and we would often wonder if most of these folks were serious about changing jobs—their cover letters and résumés were simply not getting our attention because they failed to interject any effort into their strategy for getting hired.

Hiring Managers are Overloaded in Up and Down Economies

No matter the industry in which I have worked, I have always had to contend with the constraints of too much work and not enough people to do the work. That was true when the economy was flourishing at record levels in the mid-to-late 1990s, and when it was in the basement and climbing out, as it has been over the past 24 or so months. In a booming economy, the project work arrived at a hectic pace, but hiring qualified people fast enough was always a problem. In a down economy, while reductions in force may have reduced the number of people doing the work, the workload nevertheless increased because of fewer people on the team to perform it. Add to that intensity is the fact that many companies understand the best time to push new product development is when costs are down.

The pressure to complete projects on schedule and on budget is intense in any economy, and any process that competes for the team's time and effort on Priority 1 projects is often not received with great excitement. Résumé screening and interviewing can often become one of those processes because it involves several people on the team or may involve the entire team. Because résumé screening and interviewing are intermittent processes (not part of the daily routine), sometimes they suffer from inefficiency and poor execution.

Who Extends the Offer: HR or the Hiring Manager?

In many companies, the person with the ultimate authority to extend an offer to a candidate is more often than not the hiring manager and not the HR manager or someone on the HR staff. The hiring manager, who can be a technical or non-technical person, is the individual most intimate with the details of the day-to-day responsibilities of the position that the company is trying to fill. Hiring managers have their finger on the pulse of the team, know what specific skills are required for the position, and understand the kind of personality needed to "gel" with the rest of the team.

While an HR manager or personnel consultant may screen résumés for the "best fit" candidates, in most instances it is the hiring manager that determines who gets called in for the interview. And, while the HR manager may be the person who extends the official job offer to the successful candidate, the hiring manager usually determines who that candidate is and may even dictate some of the terms of the compensation package.

If you receive a job offer and you accept it, it is likely you will report to the hiring manager directly or someone who reports to him or her. Depending on the size of the company, you may never even meet the HR person who sent you the official offer letter (unless you are being hired for a position in HR, of course).

Understanding the "Years Experience" Requirement in Job Ads

Some job ads require a certain minimum number of years experience with a particular process, methodology, or tools, or experience in a specific industry. Depending on the industry and position, that requirement may not be a hard and fast one.

Several years ago, I had a position available that required five years experience with a specific software application. One applicant wrote me complaining about that requirement, probably because he did not have the requisite number of years experience with the software tool the position demanded:

> *Does the "five years experience" requirement mean having the technical competence of a typical person with five years experience? If that's the case, then what about the person with six months or a year's experience who can do pretty cool things? What*

about someone with five years experience using a different tool but minimally competent on this one? At some point you are concerned more with an individual's potential to do good work than what he has done (and that is good, isn't it?)

I've always felt that the hardest job skills could be learned by the right person in two years or less. So, by demanding five years experience, you run the risk of hiring someone purely on the basis of the historical accident of whether they've worked at a company using a commercial tool.... Requiring "five years experience" may simply result in weeding out the younger candidates most in touch with new ways of doing things.

I disagreed with this young man's understanding of the five-years-experience requirement. For some companies, such a requirement may be a hard, non-negotiable requirement; in others, it is more of a "wish-list" item. The strength of that requirement depends on the nature of the work, but more importantly, it applies to an individual's time spent working on a *variety* of projects, solving a *variety* of problems using both standard and unique solutions with particular tools, processes, and techniques.

In my example above, individuals can not obtain that type of experience in six months or a year or two years, no matter how many "cool" things they can do with that software application—it may be cool, but does it solve a business problem? What counts more than the tools knowledge is being able to provide solutions to business problems using the tools that require their application repeatedly for many different projects and types of problems. That only comes with years of experience.

As for "weeding out the younger candidates most in touch with new ways of doing things," I did not think that was a valid point. People who work with a variety of software applications (or "tools" of any kind for that matter) to solve problems every day are usually very current with the latest tools and techniques used in the workplace. People just out of school have had much of that experience in a controlled academic environment. A writing project or programming assignment has a hard delivery date with fewer competing priorities or challenges directly affecting the project, frat parties and Rush Week notwithstanding.

In the working world (a less-controlled environment), that project is now at the mercy of design changes, project priority changes, departures of critical employees, feature additions, endless meetings, layoffs, conference calls, hard-disk crashes, and so on.

The five-years-experience requirement was a valid one. Even though some less-experienced people may have been immersed in "baptism-by-fire" work environments, it can not substitute for many years solving business problems with a variety of tools and approaches.

In some industries and professions, there is little opportunity for entry-level technical positions. Many companies have to demand a minimum number of years experience because of the fast, hit-the-ground-running, think-on-your-feet pace they have to undertake for ever-shrinking product development cycles their customers demand.

What I've Learned as a Hiring Manager

Over my 20-plus-year career in various hiring manager positions, I have been involved with hiring interns, cooperative education students, laboratory personnel, scientists and engineers with various advanced degrees, adjunct faculty candidates, and communications professionals for both permanent and contractor positions. During that time, I have reviewed well over 1,000 résumés, hundreds of cover letters and cover emails, and participated in hundreds of interviews in addition to attending training on hiring and interviewing techniques. Despite all the books, training, free information on dozens of websites, and seminars available for showing people how to write résumés and cover letters and prepare for interviews, I have come to this conclusion:

> *Most job/career seekers do not understand the*
> *strategy and tactics involved with securing a new job*
> *or career, nor do they grasp the marketing and self-*
> *promotion that is necessary to capture the attention*
> *of hiring managers before, during, and after*

21

interviews. The job/career seeker must have some understanding of the hiring manager's needs and challenges, and tailor each approach to address those concerns. The individual promoting himself/herself as the hiring manager's problem solver will be at the top of the list over anyone else with equal qualifications just looking for a job.

If you are a job/career seeker and are not having any success with securing that new job or career, you may need to revisit your approach to the task. Do you need to be more methodical in how you package yourself on paper and in person? Do you need to better anticipate what the hiring manager's world is like so you can create a memorable encounter in a cover letter or interview? Do you need to present yourself more as a problem solver looking for a new environment that offers fresh challenges, and less as someone in need of a job or career change? Empathizing with the needs and concerns of a hiring manager in a cover letter (and interview) will nearly always get that hiring manager's attention—much more so than the usual cover letter that reeks of self-adulation for past accomplishments.

A Final Word

The market is full of books, blogs, and websites on résumé writing and interviewing. These platforms offer useful advice, but there are few that provide job seekers and career changers with those tangibles and intangibles from a hiring manager's perspective sought for in qualified candidates.

As we make our way through this book, we will look at how to create a *PSKE Portfolio* that hiring managers will remember, a strategy for how to control the job interview (most other books explain how to survive a job interview, which is the wrong approach altogether), and a strategy for how to negotiate the best possible compensation package without leaving money on the table.

None of this is rocket science but it does involve intelligence gathering, creativity, and determination to help you understand which factors influence your next job or career "launch."

Over your career, you may have to adjust your strategies to the generally accepted practices of those professions and fields you wish to enter. What may work for you in one field may require adjustments to be applicable in another field. In fact, that is the reason why more than one type of résumé is used in the marketplace—to respond to the different needs across a variety of professions.

But one thing should remain fairly constant—those needs, issues, and concerns that are important to hiring managers and your ability to address them through the items in your *PSKE Portfolio*, by how well you control the interview, and in your on-the-job followthrough.

Become a keen observer of subtleties that can make a difference in being called in for an interview and being passed over without consideration. Study the job postings carefully and try to see deeper beneath the words in the ad. What peripheral skills would be needed for this particular requirement? What parallel skills do I have that are not mentioned in the ad that would separate me out from the pack of other candidates? What does this work environment look like based on the job ad information? How can I position myself to facilitate this team or company's success and to be the problem solver they are looking for? As you will discover throughout this book—especially in *Chapter 11 Postscript*—a large part of your success hinges upon your being sensitive to the various interests and priorities of others first, and your own secondarily.

Chapter 3
Developing a Strategy for Your Job or Career Change

SUPPOSE YOU WERE AN ACTOR/WRITER and had the opportunity to audition in front of some of Broadway's most famous producers. The winning audition will have his or her work produced and promoted. But there is a catch: you have to write your own brief, one-act play based on conditions that are set by the producers. For example:

- The play must be based in the cities where you have lived
- The work must reflect no more than three of your outstanding personal experiences/accomplishments
- You must have three to five years' previous experience in other Broadway productions
- You must be familiar with at least four of the following acting methods and demonstrate two during the audition:
  - Stanislavski

- o Meisner
- o Strasberg
- o Adler
- o Brecht
- o Grotowski
- o Suzuki

An audition is simply another form of job interview for people in the creative arts. So, who in their right mind would ask someone who is unfamiliar with these intricate details to write their one-act play for them? People do this all the time with résumés when they rely on a résumé-writing service or anyone else to do their work for them. There is nothing wrong with getting assistance or coaching from experts, which is the intent of this book, but you have to be aware of their limited knowledge regarding your specific job and career history. You profit long term by knowledge imparted to you by others; not by others performing that work for you.

If your résumé serves as your script for an interview, why in the world would you want someone else to write it? Your "audition" is based on the information you place in your résumé. Who should know better than you *exactly* what skills you have? Who should know better than you *exactly* how to couch your experience for a new position? Who should know better than you *exactly* how to parlay knowledge into value-add for the position for which you are applying? You should be in the driver's seat when it comes to developing your overall job or career strategy and creating the content for your cover letter and résumé.

I have a neighbor who had been between careers in the print/advertising and event-planning fields, with stints as an office manager and administrative assistant. She recently pleaded with me to rewrite her cover letter and résumé. Instead, I convinced her it would serve her efforts better if she did the work herself, but with a few suggestions from me. I assured her that this approach would help improve her chances of landing a higher paying job.

Her résumé was actually in pretty good shape. I had only a few suggestions to offer. Several weeks later, I received an email from her with her résumé attached, desperately pleading for my assistance again as she again tried to rewrite her résumé. I could see from the most recent version she sent me that she did not incorporate my suggestions from her previous version.

There were a few items on her revised résumé that were simply tasks ("menu selection", "ballroom decoration") she had completed and not explicit accomplishments tied to a bigger picture—specifically what value those tasks provided for her employer. She did not differentiate her skills from someone making minimum wage. She was not grasping the concept of "value-add" in her *Professional Accomplishments* section and therefore her résumé was destined to end up in the rejected pile.

"I know I can sell myself if I can only get in front of someone," she told me. "It's just that I have such a hard time

27

responding to their ads with a résumé and cover letter that will get me an interview."

I repeated my advice to her to rewrite her cover letter and résumé per my suggestions because in their current shape, they failed to communicate what she could do for any potential employer. I told her, "You need to step back from the cover letter and résumé to first develop a strategy for getting the interview. Put yourself in the position of the hiring manager and consider what kind of information is important to him or her." I suggested she change the "menu selection" and "ballroom decoration" tasks to something that spoke to a higher competence level and that did a better job promoting her organizational skills, multi-tasking proficiency, and delegation abilities.

She followed my suggestions, and several weeks later, received a job offer from a doctor's office for an office manager position. They were impressed with her ability to manage multiple priorities and work well with others from previous positions, and her shining personality came through during the interview, just as she had predicted.

The Job/Career Change Strategy Cycle

The formula is very simple:

Review→Reassess→Rethink→Reconstruct→ Renew (Repeat).

Figure 1 shows how this strategic cycle works to ensure your résumé reflects not only your most current professional history but parallels your objectives and goals.

Figure 1. Job/Career Change Strategy Cycle

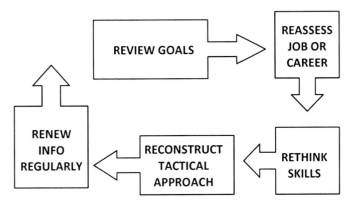

1. **Review** your current goals and aspirations and how your present job or career addresses them. Can you get there from where you are now?

2. **Reassess** your job/career to determine whether it is aligned clearly with those goals and aspirations; if you are unemployed, how did your most recent job/career align with your goals? Do you need a course adjustment or a complete change of direction?

3. **Rethink** your experience, skills, and knowledge; what do you need to do to remain in your current profession or career that will help you move closer to your goals? Or, which skills, experience, and knowledge can transfer

to other professions or industries? What other skills or knowledge do you need to acquire to move forward?

4. **Reconstruct** your tactical approach (cover letter, résumé and interview preparation) for selling yourself to hiring managers.

5. **Renew** this information on a regular basis so that your résumé and related documents reflect your current job, responsibilities, and accomplishments. The best time to look for a job is when you already have one. It is also much easier to send a current résumé instead of updating one that is years out of date—especially when the opportunity of a lifetime presents itself *immediately.*

Elements of the Job/Career Hiring Strategy Cycle

The major elements of the Job/Career Hiring Strategy Cycle are the cover letter, résumé, and interview. Additional or optional elements would include a separate list of publications, list of patents, letters of recommendation, or any other inventory of noted accomplishments that may be common to your profession or industry or the one in which you want to work. I will discuss those items separately in the chapters ahead.

Figure 2 illustrates the inter-dependability of the cover letter, résumé, and interview. The gear labeled "cover letter" is larger than the "résumé" and "interview" gears because an attention-getting cover letter means in all likelihood your résumé will be read, and if you have a knockout résumé, your chances for being called for an interview go way up.

Figure 2. Elements of the Job/Career Hiring Strategy Cycle

The success of your job-search or career-change strategy hinges upon several elements of which you have significant control:

1. How good you look on your cover letter, résumé, and other supportive documents in your *PSKE Portfolio*. Do they present you as a consummate professional? Do they truly speak to your accomplishments and abilities?

2. What others say about you (professional and/or personal references). Have you alerted your references ahead of time that they may be notified? Can those individuals attest to your best qualities?

3. How well you did in the interview session(s). Were you able to answer behavioral or situational interview

questions clearly and succinctly? Were you displaying a positive image and asking questions of the interviewers?

All three of these major elements are evaluated to assist in determining whether you will in fact receive a job offer. Obviously, with a great cover letter and résumé, excellent personal and professional references, and a positive interview, your chances increase for receiving a job offer (see **Figure 3** for a graphical representation of how these elements work together to create the *Job Offer Probability Funnel*).

Figure 3. Job Offer Probability Funnel

How you look on paper

How well you did in the interview

What others have to say about you

Probability of receiving a job offer

The three major elements of the *Job Offer Probability Funnel* rely on (1) elements of your *PSKE Portfolio*; (2) how you were perceived during the interview, and (3) what your references say about your character and your abilities. The chapters that follow will address all of these factors in more detail.

Sometimes, a company's hiring process may contain hidden intangibles you may not have control over, such as how others on the interview team think you will be a match for the corporate culture or perhaps whether your presence on the team will upset the existing "team dynamic" (the synergy the team has together). Such considerations occur with many candidates across nearly all industries, but here is an extreme example.

In one company I worked, one of the employees was granted a two-month medical leave of absence, during which time he underwent a transgender procedure. Just prior to this person's return to work, the HR department called a meeting with all employees to alert us about this upcoming change in the work environment along with a reminder of company workplace policies.

Needless to say, such a situation overturned the team dynamic (through no malicious or purposeful fault of this individual) as people tried to adjust to this "new" person in their midst who they knew for years as "Al" but now had to call "Alice." This individual later left the company through a large reduction in the workforce but found work elsewhere in an environment where no one knew of her personal background. And like a tsunami in a bathtub, it took some time for the team dynamic to return to its normal level at the former company.

While a candidate rarely may be asked directly from members of the inteview team: "Have you ever done anything to upset the team dynamic?", it may be a question one hiring manager may ask of a candidate's former hiring manager when checking on references. Needless to say, responses to such questions have to be couched very carefully.

Some companies impose other prerequisites that may be beyond your control. For example, one Silicon Valley technology company requires all prospective electrical engineering hires to have a 3.5 undergraduate or graduate grade point average (GPA), regardless of how many years' experience the candidate may possess. Such a narrow gate for otherwise qualified, experienced candidates to pass through seems to limit the calibre of more senior-level hires in the company. In fact, managers at the local offices are often thwarted in their hiring efforts as the CEO (who also screened engineering résumés) rejected very highly experienced engineers for having less than a 3.5 GPA.

For many other professions, such issues are of a lesser concern as they may have a completely different set of intangibles that have a smaller impact on the probability of your receiving a job offer.

A Final Word

Whether you arrive for an interview at corporate headquarters in a three-piece suit and a leather briefcase, or at the job site trailer dressed in work clothes with tools in hand, you have to have a strategy for getting from cover letter/résumé (or job application) to interiew to job offer. There is no "one solution fits all" approach to jobs within the same industry or profession. You must carefully consider how you should respond to each individual job posting that will best present your demonstrated expertise and ability to deliver in the future. This book will help you do that.

Hiring managers are more interested in your potential for what you *can* do rather than what you have already done, though what you have accomplished is a leading indicator of your capability to perform should you be hired. Your cover letter serves as your brochure, and your résumé is your calling card that features your skills, knowledge, and experience. The format of your résumé showcases the application of your personal intellectual property (through quantified accomplishments, such as dollars earned/saved or percent improvement, if that information is available) with each employer or through functional areas of expertise.

Chapter 4
Résumés: Your Ticket to Interview City

WHY DO WE START WITH THE RÉSUMÉ if the cover letter is the first thing a hiring manager reads? The strategy is to develop the cover letter from the high points of your résumé. That way, the two work in concert to reinforce the promotion of your skills, knowledge, and experience. If your cover letter is the "sizzle," then your résumé is the "prime rib" of your professional life because the résumé represents the meat of your skills, knowledge, accomplishments, and education that hiring managers will use to determine who gets a ticket to Interview City—and tickets are getting more difficult to come by these days.

You may be considering a job move within the same industry or profession or you may be thinking about a different career altogether. Whichever way you are leaning, you must use the résumé format that best highlights your skills, knowledge, and experience for your goals.

Résumés fall into two general categories: *reverse-chronological* and *functional*. A reverse-chronological résumé highlights your current or most recent job responsibilities and accomplishments, and works backwards in time to your first job. A reverse-chronological résumé is used for staying in the same or closely related profession or industry as your current or most recent position.

If you are interested in changing careers altogether, are a recent college graduate, have diverse work experience, or have large gaps in your employment history, then a functional résumé emphasizes your acquired expertise that can transfer to other industries or professions. The functional résumé also places less emphasis on the chronology of employment dates. Both types of résumés have much of the same information on them; the major difference is that the information is arranged in a different presentation format to accentuate your background for different purposes.

Résumés have two other aspects that you should be aware of: *content* and *presentation*, and the two work closely together to put forth the best possible representation of your professional background.

Should You Use the Services of a Résumé Writer?

I addressed this issue briefly in Chapter 2, but this is an important point that needs more elaboration. Many résumé writers are freelance writers who perhaps specialize in business writing or business communications. Some may have certifications such as *Certified Leadership & Talent Management Coach, Certified Professional Résumé Writer (CPRW), Nationally Certified Résumé Writer (NCRW),* while others may have little or no experience in career counseling or in human resources. Entrusting someone who does not have near the knowledge of your own experience as you do to write your résumé can be a risky investment. If you prefer the services of a professional résumé writer, get referrals or recommendations from others who have had hiring interviews based on a professional résumé writer's work.

An old saying seems appropriate here: "Give a man a fish, you have fed him for today. Teach a man to fish, and you have fed him for a lifetime." Having someone else write your résumé for you is the equivalent of them giving you a fish for the day. What you really want is to be fed for a lifetime by being able to write your own résumé for whatever job or career change you find yourself in today and in the future. No one knows the extent of your skills, the breadth of your experience, and the depth of knowledge better than you, and no one can express it better than you. You might need some help, but you should be responsible for writing—and rewriting—that résumé and cover letter.

Revision and polish are a necessary and hard part of the writing process; there just are no shortcuts to creating a job-grabbing cover letter and résumé. It is also much easier to commit to paper or computer screen a professional history written in your own words because you lived it and can best express it in meaningful terms to a hiring manager. That skill feeds you for a lifetime.

Who Really Looks at Résumés?

Résumé screening is the process companies use to filter out candidates who do not meet the minimum skill levels or experience requirements, or candidates who do not have the requisite education for the position from those who do. While the practice varies across the spectrum, many companies can be somewhat flexible on skill levels or experience requirements, depending on the quality of the skills and/or experience in question. Depending on the industry and position, it is sometimes more difficult for companies to allow any latitude on the educational requirement.

Some companies use employment or hiring consultants to screen résumés from applicants while others may use HR personnel for the task. Throughout most of my experience, hiring managers provide HR with the necessary requirements and prerequisites for the available position based on the overall team need to establish a competitive compensation package to start with. HR forwards to the hiring manager's attention only those résumés that meet the criteria. It streamlines the process for everyone involved and is the most efficient way to determine which candidates to call for an interview.

Hiring managers and their teams are in the best position to determine which of the filtered candidate résumés most directly address the needs of the team. Once potential interview candidates have been identified, the hiring manager may conduct a phone screen as the next filter in the process.

The phone screen is an informal conversation between the hiring manager and the candidate about previous experience or specific knowledge to determine if an invitation to an interview should be extended. A candidate who does well in a phone interview will likely be called for an in-person interview.

How to Do Well in a Phone Screen

If you have written an attention-getting résumé, chances are a hiring manager will want to next perform a phone screen. I have written off a few potential candidates from any further consideration based on poor results from a phone interview, so do not take the task lightly.

Here are a hiring manager's tips for having a successful phone screen:

- At the agreed-upon time, go into a quiet room and shut the door.
- No TV on mute (turn it off), no pets, no kids in the room with you—and turn off the computer (do not give the phone screener any excuse to think you are updating your *Facebook* page or checking email).

41

- Sit in a comfortable chair at a table or desk, or if you prefer, stand up and walk around if you have a Bluetooth headset—some individuals find it easier to communicate using body language even on a phone call (as I do).
- Have a copy of your résumé in front of you or any other documents that can help in the conversation.
- Focus on the conversation; be deliberate in your responses (no long pauses punctuated with "um...", "well, like...", "you know...", etc.)—it conveys the idea that you are not prepared or are not interested.
- Be conscious of any distracting motions or noises, such as clicking pen, tapping a pencil on a table, etc.
- Come across as the consummate professional your cover letter and résumé (or job application) implies.

Structure Your Résumé for Efficient Information Access

Interviewing candidates is not an inexpensive exercise. For example, if three candidates have been invited for an hour-long panel interview and the interview team consists of five technical people at $70/hour salary and the hiring manager at $90/hour, which is $440 in hourly wages x three candidates or $1,320 for interviewing three candidates. This cost does not include the time to screen résumés, conduct phone screens, running ads on job boards or in print periodicals, the cost of not working on revenue-generating projects for that time, or the possibility of the candidate accepting an offer from another company. Some companies may still provide air fare for out-of-town candidates, and that can also include food and lodging. Other companies may reimburse interview candidates for mileage if they drive to and from the interview location.

That said, it should be obvious that a well-designed and formatted résumé that facilitates navigation through it helps résumé screeners and hiring managers quickly find the information they need to determine whether to bring someone in for an interview. Make a résumé screener or hiring manager hunt for information on a résumé, and that candidate may likely be bypassed for an interview. I know; I have done it many times. Let the architecture and layout of your résumé be guided by the seven-second rule.

Next up: the building blocks of a reverse-chronological résumé first, and then those of a functional résumé.

Reverse-Chronological Résumé Building Blocks

Here are what I consider the standard building blocks of a reverse-chronological résumé. Every résumé should have at a *minimum* these information sections (usually in this order):

- Name and Contact Information block
- Professional Summary block
- Experience block (most recent to oldest)
- Education block (most recent to oldest)

Optional résumé building blocks would include any of the following (usually after the Education block):

- Awards block
- Certifications block
- Patents block
- Languages block
- Publications block
- Military Service block
- Miscellaneous block

Let's look at each one of these in some detail.

Name and contact information block. Placed at the top of the page, centered, left, or right—it does not matter, but ensure all information is accurate and current. If you include a URL to a personal web page (*Facebook, MySpace,* etc.), I guarantee it will get visited if your résumé makes it to a hiring manager's desk. Be sure to remove those Cancun spring break photos *and* any content that shows you in a compromising position or paints you in an unfavorable light if you are going to share that information with the world.

Professional Summary block. This short one-paragraph block is a summary of your skills, knowledge, and experience that has a promotional tone to it. NOTE: This is NOT an "Objectives" section.

Experience block. Start the listing with your most recent employer. Hiring managers want to see employment date range, employer name, your job title/function, brief description of duties and responsibilities (short paragraph or bullet list). If you can assign a dollar figure to any initiative, project, or program with which you were directly involved that generated revenue, cost savings, or percent improvement, by all means include it. If you have more than 10 to 12 years of experience, a one-line description for those positions older than that will suffice. Be sure to account for any gaps in your employment history; it will not count against you nearly as much as lying about it.

Education block. Start with your most recent degree or highest level of education. Hiring managers want to see school name, years attended, and degrees awarded or course of study pursued. If you do not include any degree designation (A.A. B.A, B.S., M.S, etc.), the assumption is that you did not graduate with that degree. Do not include your GPA here. If you were asked to include it, place it in your cover letter instead. Omit anything on a résumé that could negate your chances of getting an interview.

Optional Information Blocks

Awards/Honors information block. If you have garnered any employer awards for your participation in work projects or programs, include them in this block. Do not include service awards (5-, 10-, 20-year employee awards)—you just showed up for work to get those.

Certification/License block If you have taken and passed exams for any kind of certifications or licenses that relate to your job responsibilities, include it in this block. Certifications and licenses testify to a certain level of knowledge and proficiency that can be a deciding factor on whether you get placed on the short list for an interview.

Patent information block. Such information shows a potential employer your ability to create product solutions that improve a design or manufacturing process that results in greater efficiency or lower cost. Many companies pay patent awards—some as high as five figures, depending on the value of the patent. While you can provide a line-item listing of patent awards on your résumé, a more detailed document would be a great addition to your *PSKE Portfolio*.

A *Patent information* block on a résumé might look something like this:

- U.S. Patent #543210, **Method for Predicting Dither Error in CMYK Color Processing**, issued September 2002.
- U.S. Patent #579235, **Algorithm for Digital Image Compression**, issued September 2003.
- U.S. Patent Pending, **Enhancing Digital Video Resolution Using Magneto-Optics**, filed May 2005.

Foreign language information block. Speaking and writing a foreign language can open many doors with a prospective employer. If you can speak, write, and/or read another language, be sure to indicate your fluency level with each type of communication (novice/conversational/fluent).

Publications block. If you have had articles published in professional (peer-reviewed) journals or industry magazines (or websites), or have had papers published in conference proceedings, add them to this block, but only if you have had six to eight or fewer published. For more than eight publications, a sentence that states "A complete list of publications is available on request" will suffice. Just ensure you have that separate list available in your *PSKE Portfolio* should a hiring manager ask to see it.

Here is an example of a *Publications* block, where the publications are arranged by subject or field.

Engineering/IT Technical Papers (1987-1993)

"Using Deionized Water as a Replacement for CFCs in Cleaning High-Purity Stainless Steel Tubing for Use in Semiconductor Manufacturing Cleanrooms," presented at the 1993 Pure Water Conference and published in the *Journal*.

"The Distributed Computing Environment in the Earth Sciences," presented at the 1987 Synercom User's Group Meeting and published in the *Transactions*.

Earth and Space Sciences Technical Papers (1978-1986)

"Extraterrestrial Catastrophic Events: Implications for Natural Resource Exploitation and Their Effect on the Geologic Column," keynote paper presented at the 1986 American Association of Petroleum Geologists (AAPG) Annual Convention/Symposium on Astrogeology, also published in the *AAPG Astrogeology Anthology*.

"Lyles Ranch Field, South Texas: Production from an Astrobleme?" Presented at the 1985 GCAGS Annual Meeting and published in the Transactions; also published in the Oil and Gas Journal (April, 1985).

"Discriminant Function Analysis as a Technique for Differentiating Basaltic Magmas by the Presence of Strategic Elements," presented at the 1985 Conference on Geomathematics, Johnson Space Center, and published in the *Transactions*.

Military service block. If you are a veteran, state so here along with all the pertinent information (branch of service, rank, discharge date, etc.). When entering the civilian workforce, the details of your exact military duties likely will not be needed on your résumé because you will have already translated those duties into marketable skills, knowledge, and experience elsewhere. Do include the basic information that shows your dates of service.

- **U.S. Army National Guard, El Paso, TX**
  Squad Leader/Sergeant (2005 - 2009)
- **U.S. Army, Wiesbaden, Germany**
  Team Leader/Sergeant (2000 - 2005); Honorable Discharge

Miscellaneous block. Mention civic/community service activities you are involved with here, such as Elks, homeowner association officer, or other volunteer service, especially if you lack job experience. Keep aligned to those items that reinforce the image you are trying to present to the hiring manager. Do not include religious activities on your résumé unless you are interviewing for a job/career with a religious institution or church-affiliated organization, or mention any activity involvement that may cast concern on your professional standing.

Functional Résumé Building Blocks

Many of the building blocks for a functional résumé are the same as for the reverse-chronological résumé—they are in a different order because they have slightly different purposes. I have found that including *Optional Information* blocks ahead of the *Education* block works very well for candidates because the purpose of the functional résumé is to transfer expertise to a different profession or industry. Much of that know-how is incorporated into such specialized areas as publications, patents, awards, certifications, etc. Many hiring managers evaluating a functional résumé consider the information in these supportive sections as having higher priority than the *Education* block.

Here are the major information blocks of a functional résumé:

- Name and contact information block
- Professional Summary block
- Functional Area blocks (more than one)
- Experience block
- Optional information block
- Education block

Name and contact information block. Same suggestions as for reverse-chronological résumé.

Professional Summary block. Same suggestions as for the reverse-chronological résumé.

Functional Area blocks. The specific accomplishments you attained at each job fall under functional disciplines that capture your skill, knowledge, and experience. For example, your demonstrated skill with managing multiple complex tasks, projects, and people would suggest a "Project Management" functional block, or your ability to successfully resolve customer issues would suggest a "Customer Relations and Support" functional block. Review the functional résumé examples to see how to assemble information for *Functional Area* blocks.

Experience block. Unlike the *Experience* block on a reverse-chronological résumé, here you simply list dates of employment, employer name, and job title. Those individual accomplishments listed under each employer on a reverse-chronological résumé show up as one-line items (and slightly reworded) under the *Functional Area* block.

Optional information block. See Chapter 6 for the types of information that would be placed here.

Education block. Same suggestions as for the reverse-chronological résumé. For many hiring managers evaluating transferable expertise, the *Education* block may not provide as much "data" and value as does content from the *Optional Information* block.

10 Items Most Hiring Managers Don't Want to See on or Accompanying a Résumé

While there are certainly important items every résumé must have, the flip side is also true: that some information really does not belong on a résumé. Most of these examples should be obvious; however, it never fails that most résumé screeners and hiring managers will receive résumés containing the following information:

1. **Objective section.** Avoid including an "Objective" section on your résumé. Forget what other authors write about creating an awe-inspiring *Objectives* section on your résumé—it is self-serving, states the obvious (you need a job), and takes up precious space on the page. Instead, use the cover letter to sell the hiring manager on your objective—which is to *help the hiring manager solve problems;* **not** to hear about *you and your needs.* Here are some actual examples of useless, trite *Objectives* from résumés I have received for a senior-level technical writer full-time, permanent position—none of which addressed the needs of the hiring manager:

    *   "To obtain a technical writing or publications management position in an interesting environment"
    *   "Seeking a technical training or technical writing engagement in which to apply my strong adult learning and communication skills" (for the same position that

51

did not have "adult learning" or "technical training" in the job description)

- "A contract writing position with a software or hardware company" (that's as far as I needed to read)

2. **Any coursework that did not lead to certification, license, or a degree.** Hiring managers know that listing course after course of study that did not lead to a degree, certification, or license is a tactic to deflect attention away from an insufficient or incomplete education history. That is not a problem if the position does not require a college degree or for specialized training in the military. Hiring managers in many professions and industries are more interested in your responsibilities and accomplishments in the real-world rather than a controlled environment that is characteristic of individual classes, two-day workshops, or week-long seminars. Sometimes the real world does not break for lunch, quitting time, spring break, or vacations.

3. **Having only one version of your résumé.** You have many facets to your experience that one résumé version simply can not address. Tailor your skill set, experience, and knowledge to the requirements and duties of the position to which you are applying because many if not most job postings contain more stringent prerequisites than what a company will actually accept. If you are using only one version of your résumé, you can appear desperate because there is no focus on the position for which you are applying.

In fact, if your experience matches a particular skillset or experience in a job posting, copy that list from the job posting to your résumé and address how your experience, skills, and knowledge meet those criteria.

4. **Not sending a cover letter with your résumé.** Not including a cover letter when one is requested in an ad almost guarantees your not being considered at all for the available position by many hiring managers. Keep it to one page or less, and sell yourself as the hiring manager's problem solver. Make reviewers want to read your résumé to confirm how good your cover letter says you are. Cover letters should take on the tone of "I understand your challenges and here's what I can do for you" and not the usual "here's why I'm so great" or "here's what I've done" slant.

5. **Mixing too many job titles in the résumé contact information block.** If you want to add a job title after your name in the *Contact information* block at the top of your résumé, go ahead. But adding more than one title, such as "Software Programmer/Web Developer/Graphics Designer" just dilutes your primary strength. Instead, use separate résumés that highlight each of the different skill sets, achievements, and responsibilities for different positions.

6. **Including hobbies on your résumé.** Save it for the interview, but only if an interviewer raises the topic; otherwise, it is more appropriate as coffee pot conversation

CONFESSIONS OF A HIRING MANAGER

after you have the job. You may like to go deer hunting or raise chinchillas, but if the hiring manager interviewing you is a card-carrying member of *People for the Ethical Treatment of Animals (PETA)*, you might have just disqualified yourself, but you will never know the real reason you never got the call for an interview. Why include anything on your résumé that reduces your chances for getting that job or career you want?

7. **Using a narrative style for your résumé.** Yes, I have received résumés that read like the opening chapter of a bad novel. I once received a résumé from a law school graduate who was responding to a job posting for a legal editor that began, "John Doe has always been one to finish what he started, ever since birth..." That was as far as I needed to read. There is no place for such ill-informed, unprofessional drivel on a résumé.

8. **Doing/sending anything other than what was requested in the job posting or phone screen.** Do not send transcripts, copies of articles you have written, Ph.D. dissertations or a working prototype of some gadget unless you were asked to do so. A hiring manager colleague of mine once received a free unsolicited stinging critique of the company's website from a job applicant, who had no idea that the hiring manager was heavily involved in that project. The applicant was called for an interview for the web developer position, but the arrogance that was evident

in his website critique spilled over to the interview, just as the hiring manager suspected it would. He was not hired.

9. **Sending your résumé anyway if you do not meet the minimum requirements.** If you really believe you have something you can offer the company, then tailor your cover letter and résumé to best highlight the match between their needs and your skill set. But understand that you likely will be disappointed if what they need and what you offer does not match.

When I was one of the hiring managers for an e-Commerce software development company, we needed technical writers with some basic knowledge of the Java and C++ programming languages. I received a few reverse-chronological résumés from people who had many years of programming experience with submarine sonar systems and Patriot missile batteries, but they had none of the specific software language knowledge we needed. It appeared they had just one version of their résumé and it was the wrong one (they should have used a functional résumé to highlight their transferable skills and experience, not that it would have helped for the position that was available at this company).

Sometimes, desperation just runs amok when folks are looking for a job. The ad in **Figure 4** ran on a local job bank website for technical writers. It states clearly that résumés that did not meet the prerequisites would not be considered for the contract position. Nevertheless, I received more than 30 résumés—*none* of which met the job prerequisites. The division manager told me he had funds to hire a contractor, but that I had a week to find someone; otherwise, the funds would have to be diverted to other projects with a financial need.

Figure 4. Tech Writer Ad (Original)

ORIGINAL POSTING

Closed 7/7/06 – Senior Technical Writer/Editor

Job Type: Contract

Duration: 12 months

Duties: Revise/edit microprocessor design specs, developer manuals, API documentation

Requirements: Looking for strong candidates with 3 to 5 years experience who can hit the ground running documenting microprocessor/DSP specifications, developer manuals, PCB board design guides, and API documentation.

Only candidates with 3-5 years experience documenting microprocessor architecture and design specs will be considered for this position.

Must have advanced/expert-level skills with FrameMaker, Acrobat, Visio

Need an individual who has a sense of project urgency, sense of project ownership, and can balance value-add technical writing/ editing skills with organizational publishing requirements

Salary: Competitive contractor rates

Contact: J.T. Kirk

Additional Info: Due to the immediate and critical need, résumés received without the requisite experience and skills will not be considered. Please attach resume and cover letter to email or fax both. NO PHONE CALLS PLEASE.

I reposted a revised version of the ad in **Figure 5**.

Figure 5. Tech Writer Ad (After Rewrite)

Revised Posting 7/16/06 Repost of Senior Technical Writer/Editor from 7/7/06

Job Type: Contract

Duration: Up to 12 months

Duties: Revise/edit microprocessor design specs, developer manuals, API documentation

Requirements: If you can answer YES to these potential interview questions, then forward your cover letter and résumé to me:

1. Can you read binary and hexadecimal numbers?
2. Do you know the difference between a UART and DUART?
3. Do you know the difference between Sleep and Drowsy mode? What about bit, byte, word?
4. Do you know the difference between a CPU and peripheral?
5. Can you read register tables?
6. Do you have 7+ years technical writing experience, 3 to 5 of which MUST have been with documenting microprocessor architecture and design specifications?

This position requires editing and revising electrical engineering content using advanced FrameMaker skills with conditional text and using version control software.

Salary: Competitive contractor rates

Contact: J.T. Kirk

Additional Info: DO NOT REAPPLY TO THIS POSITION if you sent your résumé between July 7th and July 15th. THIS IS A REPOST FOR THE SAME POSITION. Attach cover letter and résumé to email or fax both. NO PHONE CALLS PLEASE.

Tips: (1) Sell me in your cover letter why I should look at your résumé; (2) Design your résumé to ADDRESS THE REQUIREMENTS OF THE POSITION (in other words, don't sell me on your RoboHELP, HTML, software skills, training curriculum development, web design skills, database design skills, etc. because it's NOT WHAT WE NEED). If you do not have the requisite skills, experience, or knowledge, you will not be considered for the position.

In the revised ad, I even give prospective candidates information on how to get my attention. I received six résumés from this ad, and of those, we invited two candidates for interview, but we hired neither.

As luck would have it, at the end of the week, I got a call from a former colleague looking for a new contract, so we brought her onboard for the one-year assignment (a diving end-zone catch with time running out). Some people had a difficult time dealing with the rejection: I received several irate emails from applicants who were upset that their résumés were not considered for the position even though their experience did not align with the company's needs. One candidate stated he would never work for me because of the wording in the restated ad.

10. **Including any project or item on your résumé that would detract from your focus.** If you list specific projects on which you have worked, they must testify to your being the consummate professional you are purporting to be. Again, focus is the operative term. If you are applying for a position as a financial writer for an industry magazine, including *The Teletubbies Tell Time Coloring Book* project on your résumé may not be a smart move (actual example), but if you are applying for an editor position with a children's magazine, it makes perfect sense as it highlights your experience (generally) with editorial responsibilities for a children's project.

Do Not Turn Your Résumé into a Work of Fiction

The temptation is always present to push the envelope of truth about your employment history on a résumé. Resist it because you will likely be found out sooner or later. Blatant falsehoods not only brand you as unqualified, but you could also be called an unqualified *liar*.

CareerBuilder conducted a survey of hiring managers about the lies and tall tales they have seen on résumés, and here are their Top 10:

1. A candidate claimed to be a member of the Kennedy clan.
2. An applicant invented a school that did not exist.
3. An applicant submitted a résumé with someone else's photo inserted into the document.
4. An applicant claimed to be a member of Mensa (the society for people with an IQ of 140 or higher)
5. An applicant claimed to have worked for the hiring manager at another company, but never had.
6. An applicant claimed to be the CEO of a company when he was actually an hourly employee.
7. An applicant listed military experience dating back to before he was born.
8. An applicant included samples of work, which were actually those of the interviewer.
9. An applicant claimed to be Hispanic when he was 100% Caucasian.

10. An applicant claimed to have been a professional baseball player when he never was.

The one fact that all of these bogus claims have in common is that *they can be verified easily* thanks to the Internet.

It has never been easier to check credentials, so says the Association of Certified Fraud Examiners, which provides training, written and graded assessments and certification for fraud examiners. The organization teaches foreign and domestic law-enforcement agents, auditors, insurance investigators, bank examiners, hiring managers, anti-terrorism investigators and others how to detect all types of financial fraud and identity theft. One axiom they promote in training: most people get caught sooner or later, and many are found out during the interview process simply by patterns of body language that are consistent with exaggerating the truth and outright falsehoods.

The short-term gain never makes up for the long-term consequences, whether it is a bogus claim on a résumé or embezzling money.

Reverse-Chronological Résumé: Single Field/Single Experience

This résumé is from someone whose entire professional work experience has been in one field (academia).

DIANE R. SMITH

12345 MAIN STREET

MINNEAPOLIS, MN 55404

612.555.5555

DIANESMITH@EMAIL.COM

SUMMARY OF SKILLS   ①

Name, phone number, and email are all that are needed today

- 16 years experience as Director of Tra
- Certified and experienced facilitator for Myers-Briggs Type I and II.
- Highly skilled in writing, design, training and delivery of employee development services.

PROFESSIONAL EXPERIENCE   ②

University of Minnesota, Minneapolis, MN

Manager, Training and Development, 1998 to present

- Supervised professional staff of 20 and support staff of 5.
- Designed and implemented new online system of training opportunities for U of MN employees.
- Improved approach to customer service, raising customer satisfaction by 30% over 2 years.
- Created formal Work-Life Initiative for employees and relocated spouses and partners.
- Provided professional consultation for administrative departments.

University of St. Thomas, St. Paul, MN

Manager, Training and Development, 1993 to 1998

- Conducted thorough needs assessment; designed and implemented professional development program for staff.
- Facilitated workshops and orientation programs for new employees.
- Marketed training services to department chairs and supervisors.
- Received Service Award from President of the University.

Coe College, Cedar Rapids, IA
Training Specialist, 1989 to 1993
- Researched, designed and implemented new employee orientation program.
- Revised and presented numerous workshops to employees.

EDUCATION

University of Minnesota, Minneapolis, MN
Master of Arts, Human Resource Development, 1995
University of Iowa, Iowa City, IA
Bachelor of Arts, Business Administration, 1985

This résumé clearly presents the essentials for quick perusal: *Summary of Skills, Professional Experience,* and *Education.* Résumés that document experience in a single field or industry are most often one to two pages in length.

After the contact information block, we have:

① **Summary of Skills:** Diane provides a brief high-level summary of her professional skills so we can see quickly the big picture of her training and development experience.

② **Professional Experience:** Diane develops her accomplishments list using parallel structure of "action" verbs (*supervised, designed and implemented, improved, created, provided*).

③ **Education:** Simply stated, showing her Masters and Bachelors degrees and dates earned.

This simple résumé has most of the elements that would be important to a hiring manager at a university. Some hiring managers/HR managers believe that a statement about references being "available on request" is unnecessary; regardless, ensure your *PSKE Portfolio* includes a readily available list of references you can produce when asked.

Functional Résumé: College Graduate with Experience in a Field Different from Degree

John Doe
1234 Main Street
Anytown, Anystate 98765
651.555.5555
jdoe@gmail.com

Excellent Summary of Qualifications— short, to the point

Don't need so much contact information

Summary of Qualifications

Experienced manager of academic scientific laboratories. Recognized by peers and professors for success in standardizing procedures to ensure quality scientific work, and in mentoring students conducting laboratory experiments.

Professional Skills

Leadership/Management

Don't really need to lead lists with action-oriented verbs in a functional résumé

- Managed laboratory equipment and
- Negotiated contracts and discounts decrease in supply expenses
- Coordinated inter-department laboratory activities
- Interviewed, supervised and trained a staff of five; increased staff retention rate
- Presented and taught scientific methods, techniques and safety standards to staff and students
- Organized and directed the transfer of laboratory equipment and supplies to remote class sites

63

Laboratory

- Designed and performed scientif| Don't really need to
- Conducted protein analyses inclu| lead lists with action-
  chromatography, HPLC, Immuno| oriented verbs in a phoresis,
  Western blots and enzymatic ass| functional résumé
- Conducted DNA analyses including plasmid preparation, making
  probe, agarose gel electrophoresis, and southern blots analysis.
- Prepared, grew and harvested polyclonal antibodies
- Maintained a complex breeding colony of 225 mice
- Worked with livestock, poultry, rodents, reptiles, amphibians and non-
  human primates.

Writing/Technical

- Wrote, edited laboratory, safety and teaching assistant manuals
- Engaged in creative problem solving in a fast-paced environment
- Utilized software including Excel, Word, Edora, Powerpoint, Filemaker
  Pro, Netscape, PeopleSoft, SPSS

Professional Experience

> Single employer,
> but several
> positions with
> that employer

The University of Texas, Austin, TX 1989 to present
Laboratory Services Coordinator (1995 to present)
College of Biological Sciences

Senior Laboratory Technician, Biochemistry (1992 to 1995)
Department of Veterinary Pathobiology
Department of Therapeutic Radiology
Department of Medicine

> **Placing Awards**
> **before Education**
> **stresses transferable**
> **skills and expertise—**
> **smart move for a**
> **functional résumé**

Laboratory Animal Care Technician (1989 to 1992)
Research Animal Resources

Awards and Recognition

- Letter of commendation for excellence in coordinating the genetics
  laboratory
- Service Award from the College of Biological Sciences, The University
  of Texas

Education

The University of Texas, Austin, TX
Bachelor of Arts, 1988
Major: Middle Eastern Studies

Currently completing work towards Bachelor's degree in Sociology, Law, Criminology and Deviance. Expect to graduate in 2005.

Single Field/Multiple Experience Résumé

This next reverse-chronological résumé example illustrates multiple experience in a single field (electrical engineering). I modified the presentation (font and size) to facilitate reading for the book format but the content is unchanged.

> Objective: USELESS information—how does this address the hiring manager's issues?

ERNIE ENGINEER
eengineer@hotmail.com
(512) 555-0987

JOB OBJECTIVE: To obtain a challenging Test Engineering position with a dynamic high technology company.

> Professional Summary does good job of capturing various expertise over his career

PROFESSIONAL SUMMARY

Successful Test Application Engineer with diverse engineering experience in the Semiconductor and ATE industries. A high-energy, versatile professional with a strong track record for meeting aggressive project objectives.

- Experienced designing Analog Mixed Signal, Precision Audio, RF and Digital load boards for high volume production testing
- Expertise developing efficient turn key test programs for Mixed Signal, Precision Audio, RF, and Digital
- Proven ability to troubleshoot

> Too many unnecessary capitalized noun phrases

- Program management and project leadership skills
- Ability to master complex technical material quickly and thoroughly
- Experienced at working productively on cross-functional teams

PROFESSIONAL EXPERIENCE

COMPANY A, City, State
1996 to 2009
Senior Staff Applications Engineer
Develop creative solutions to cutting-edge test problems for Mixed Signal, RF, Analog and Digital devices.

> **Too many unnecessary capitalized noun phrases**

- Develop hardware and software for the testing of a wide variety of consumer devices including Digital Audio, ADCs, DACs, Wireless Networks, Tri-band Transceivers, DVD Controllers, Graphics, Digital Signal Processors, Network Processors, Microprocessors, Microcontrollers, and Serdes Buses.
- Developed new multi-site test technique 35% and helped save one of our biggest competitor
- Developed initial test solutions and provided training for multiple new customers. Most successful were the ATI and Cirrus Logic accounts, resulting in approximately $450M and $150M in sales.
- Developed new test tools on the Diamond product for use in Failure Analysis labs. This opened a new market for the product line, which was previously only used in production.
- Authored application notes and training materials used by our customers and field applications training to customers around the

> **Hiring managers like this kind of information**

> **Good use of parallel structure in bullet list by starting each item with action verb**

COMPANY B, City, State
1988 to 1994
Digital Design Specialist
Provided applications and sales support for a specialist sales team focused at digital design.

- Assisted customers in testing and characterizing their new designs.
- Gave product demonstrations and presentations to customers differentiating the capabilities of Tektronix instruments versus our competitors. Grew the business for these products year after year despite having prices that were as much as four times that of our biggest competitor.
- Researched and qualified new areas of business for expansion of this market.

COMPANY C, City, State
Senior Marketing Applications Engineer
1984 to 1986
Provided technical marketing support to worldwide sales team. Actively, participated in development of sales and marketing strategies. Identified new market segments, generated new product proposals and coordinated the development efforts of both the hardware and software engineering teams.

> **Good use of parallel structure in bullet list by starting each item with action verb**

- Conducted customer and market research to define the product roadmap.
- Wrote marketing proposals and ROI justifications for both software and hardware products.
- Participated in cross-functional product development teams.
- Developed initial application solutions for new products.
- Provided product training for the sales and field application groups.
- Generated marketing literature and application notes for use by the worldwide sales force.

Telecommunications Applications Supervisor
1982 to 1984
While actively developing Telecom applications, I supervised a team of 4 Applications Engineers for Telecom products group.

- Developed new system instrumentation, as well as, customer specific hardware/software test solutions.
- Specified and developed user syntax used on new Telecom instrumentation.

- This group was responsible for **40%** of Series 80 sales during that time frame.

TECHNICAL SKILLS

> Nice, concise table format for identifying technical skills according to the various functions of those skills/tools

Programming Languages:	
Operating Systems:	Linux, Unix, Windows
Software Development Tools:	ClearCase (source control and bug tracking), SlickEdit
Design Tools:	DesignWorks, Multisim
Mathematics:	Statistical Analysis, DSP (sampling, modulation, noise)

EDUCATION

Bachelor of Science in Electrical Engineering Technology
DeVry Institute of Technology, Phoenix, AZ

> **Most engineering jobs require a bachelor's degree at a minimum. This individual's expertise collectively paints a picture of a highly qualified engineer for the open position.**

Overall, this is a fairly good example of technical résumé. The presentation of the information follows a repeatable pattern (company, location, dates, brief general description followed by bulleted list), and the architecture of the information helps lead the eye through the various context blocks (*Professional Summary, Professional Experience, Technical Skills,* and *Education*), though the *Objective* section is a non-essential entry. The overuse of unnecessary capitalization suggests poor grammatical skills. Such an issue might be a minor problem if part of the job description for the position required good grammatical skills for writing product specifications or customer documentation. The amount of weight placed on such a requirement varies from one engineering team (or company) to the next, often depending on whether a technical editorial or technical publications team is available to provide documentation support.

Functional Résumé: Multiple Field/Multiple Experience Résumé

Stan is an outstanding technical communications professional who offers a variety of technical experience in several capacities as a team member, individual contributor, and manager. His functional résumé is one of the best examples of a candidate with many years experience across multiple disciplines and industries.

See note about action words in lists**	Stan Smith (617) 555-3321 stansmith@yahoo.co	This summary is a good length for someone with 23 years experience in a variety of disciplines

SUMMARY OF QUALIFICA

More than 23 years of demonstrated technical and scientific communication project management leadership for a portfolio of employers and clients in software development, microprocessor design, industrial automation, eCommerce, and the earth and space sciences. Knowledgeable, results-oriented, value-add solutions provider with a broad range of portable business, technology, communications, leadership, and management skills to help achieve on-time and within-budget project/business objectives.

CORE DISCIPLINES

Technical Communications/Publications

> Stan highlights (in bold) quantified achievements

- Documentation Usability / Human Factors (microprocessors, microcontrollers, workstations, programmable controllers, storage area networks, and process control software)
- Technical Publication Project Management
- XML-derived Documentation Planning, Analysis, Management
- Database Publishing Design and Coordination **($2.3 million saved in publishing costs over 3 years for division)**

Project Management

- Marketing Communications Program Initiatives
- Documentation Distribution Process Improvement **(66% efficiency improvement to the documentation development process)**
- Documentation Development Methodology Efficiency Improvement **(20% process efficiency improvement)**

Quality Initiatives

- Process Improvement Initiative Management (ISO 9000, CPI, Six Sigma)

Instruction/Instructional Design

- Adjunct Faculty Lecturer (Dept of Natural Sciences and Mathematics)
- Training Database Design/Development **(savings of $75,000 annually)**
- Video Training Modules Design/Creation

EMPLOYMENT HISTORY

8/00-present:	Acme Semiconductor, Boston, MA
Title:	Technical Publications Project Manager
3/99 – 8/00:	Integrated eCommerce Concepts, Inc., Dallas, TX
Title:	Manager, Information Development
11/94 – 11/98:	Big Name Electronics, Schaumberg, IL
Title:	Information Development Project Manager
1991 – 1994:	Stan Smith Technical Communications, Dallas, TX
Title:	Technical and Scientific Communications Consultant

1988 -1991:	Clayton Controls, Dallas, TX
Title:	Communications Project Leader
1986 - 1988	SysComm Technology, Inc., SugarLand, TX
Title:	Technical Writer/Editor; Oil and Gas Mapping Division
1984 - 1986	Sweetwater Resources, Inc. Houston, TX
Title:	Exploration Geologist/Project Manager
1981 - 1982	University of Houston Downtown College Houston, TX
Title:	Adjunct Faculty Member (part time)
1980 - 1984	Big 3 Petroleum Company, Division, Houston, TX
Title:	Frontier Area Projects Sr. Geologist
1978 – 1980	Atlantic Oceanographic -Mete
Title:	Research Geological Oceanog

Publications, Awards, and Certifications help demonstrate Stan's transferable expertise

PUBLICATIONS

Extensive publication list available on request.

AWARDS

- U.S. Dept. of Commerce Special Achievement Award for Scientific Contributions in the Field 1979-80
- Big 3 Oil Company Extra Performance Award, 1982
- Clayton Controls Quality Award, 1989, for Titan System Documentation
- Big Name Electronics OGM Award, 1995
- Big Name Electronics Silver Quill Award, 1995, 1996, 1997, 1998 for Publication Excellence
- Big Name Electronics Gold Quill Award, 1998
- Big Name Electronics CEO Award for Volunteerism, 1997

CERTIFICATIONS

- Information Mapping
- ISO 9000 Level II and III Documentation
- Project Risk Analysis and Response (through Project Management Institute and George Washington University)
- Managing Projects in Large Organizations (through Project Management Institute and George Washington University)

LANGUAGES

Former foreign language major

- Spanish-Fluent (read/write/speak)
- French-semi-conversational only
- Italian-semi-conversational only

EDUCATION

State University, FL; Bachelor of Science, Geology/Geophysics (1978)
University of State, TX; Master of Science, Geochemistry

REFERENCES

Professional and personal references provided upon request.

> ****Functional résumés listing functional areas of expertise do not have to begin with action-style verbs. Use of noun phrases on a functional résumé implies expertise in the areas under each functional category.**

Reverse Chronological Résumé: Multiple Field/Multiple Experience Résumé

Next is Stan's reverse-chronological résumé, which contains much of the same content as the functional version. In Chapter 5, you will see how Stan's cover letter represents the highlights of his résumé, along with a few other details. I will skip highlighting Stan's reverse-chronological résumé version as it is obvious how he rearranged the résumé content.

When your *PSKE Portfolio* consists of three or more *different* representations of the *same* information content (cover letter, two kinds of résumés), you are in a very good position to be able to speak at length about your skills, knowledge, and experience in any interview situation.

Stan Smith
(617) 555-3321
stansmith@yahoo.com

SUMMARY OF QUALIFICATIONS

More than 23 years of demonstrated technical and scientific communication project management leadership for a portfolio of employers and clients in software development, microprocessor design, industrial automation, eCommerce, and the earth and space sciences. Knowledgeable, results-oriented, value-add solutions provider with a broad range of portable business, technology, communications, leadership, and management skills to help achieve on-time and within-budget project/business objectives.

PROFESSIONAL EXPERIENCE

8/00-present: Acme Semiconductor, Boston, MA
Title: Technical Publications Project Manager
Duties: *Manage team of technical writers and editors supporting microprocessor design/architecture specs and application engineering user documentation*

- Managed team of technical writers creating microprocessor design specs, architecture specs, and user documentation for several families
- Supported storage area network engineering team by providing user documentation (for software applications)
- Managed the company Technical Communications Council, consisting of technical writers and editors across all company geographies
- Taught basic and advanced FrameMaker classes to engineers
- Created video training tutorials of FrameMaker functions using Camtasia

3/99 – 8/00:   Integrated eCommerce Concepts, Inc. Dallas, TX
Title: Manager, Information and Proposal Development
Duties: *Manage team of technical writers and editors in 3 cities and manage editing of eCommerce proposals*

- Created user documentation for complex eCommerce software applications

- Managed team of technical writers and editors in Dallas, Austin, and Cape Canaveral
- Created proposal development process and written proposals that generated **$20 million in contract/ joint-venture awards in 2 years**

11/94 – 11/98: Big Name Electronics, Schaumberg, IL
Title: Information Development Project Manager
Duties: *Managed team of technical writers supporting applications engineering and design engineering groups for variety of microprocessor products*

- Assisted with creation of sector-wide database publishing initiative that **saved $2.3 million in publishing costs over 3 years**
- Managed team of technical writers supporting several microprocessor product families
- Led/participated in formal process improvement initiatives (CPI, Six Sigma)
- Co-designed training database resulting in a **savings of $75,000 annually**
- Improved documentation development methodology using Information Mapping, resulting in **20% process efficiency improvement**
- Developed system for simultaneous delivery of documentation on various media, resulting in **66% documentation delivery efficiency improvement**

1991 – 1994: Stan Smith Technical Communications, Dallas, TX
Title: Technical and Scientific Communications Consultant
Duties: *Self-employed consultant/contractor providing various technical, scientific, and marketing communications services to a variety of clients*

1988 -1991: Clayton Controls, Dallas, TX
Title: Communications Project Leader
Duties: *Team lead on assigned marcom and technical communications projects supporting process control software and automation systems*

- Worked with graphic designers, programmers, and engineers to create various marketing and technical publications supporting process control automation computer systems, programmable controllers, workstations, and associated software
- Facilitated Total Quality teams onsite
- Led effort for creating Level II ISO 9000 documentation (company **received certification on first audit attempt**)

1986 - 1988   SysComm Technology, Inc., SugarLand, TX
Title: Technical Writer/Editor; Oil and Gas Mapping Division
Duties: *Created technical and marketing communications collateral in support of geomapping software applications*

1984 - 1986   Sweetwater Resources, Inc. Houston, TX
Title: Exploration Geologist/Project Manager
Duties: *Responsible for creating drillable oil and gas prospects in the upper Texas Gulf Coast; well site geological analysis*

1981 - 1982   University of Houston Downtown College Houston, TX
Title: Adjunct Faculty Member (part time)
Duties: *Taught "Fundamentals of Petroleum Exploration and Production" to undergraduate students*

1980 - 1984   Big 3 Petroleum Company, Division, Houston, TX
Title: Frontier Area Projects Sr. Geologist
Duties: *Responsible for geological, geophysical, and geochemical assessment of the hydrocarbon potential off the U.S. Atlantic Seaboard*

1978 – 1980   Atlantic Oceanographic -Meteorological Labs, Miami, FL
Title: Research Geological Oceanographer
Duties: *Various marine geological research in laboratory and on board research ships in the Gulf of Mexico, offshore U.S. East Coast, Georges Bank, South Atlantic, and Indian Ocean*

EDUCATION

State University, FL; Bachelor of Science, Geology/Geophysics (1978)
University of State, TX; Master of Science, Geochemistry

PUBLICATIONS

Extensive publication list available on request.

AWARDS

- U.S. Dept. of Commerce Special Achievement Award for Scientific Contributions in the Field 1979-80
- Big 3 Oil Company Extra Performance Award, 1982
- Clayton Controls Quality Award, 1989, for Titan System Documentation
- Big Name Electronics OGM Award, 1995
- Big Name Electronics Silver Quill Award, 1995, 1996, 1997, 1998 for Publication Excellence
- Big Name Electronics Gold Quill Award, 1998
- Big Name Electronics CEO Award for Volunteerism, 1997

CERTIFICATIONS

- Information Mapping
- ISO 9000 Level II and III Documentation
- Project Risk Analysis and Response (through Project Management Institute and George Washington University)
- Managing Projects in Large Organizations (through Project Management Institute and George Washington University)

LANGUAGES

Former foreign language major
Linguistic ability (1=little to none; 5=fluent)

- Spanish (read=3; write=2; speak=3)
- French (read=1; write=1; speak=2)
- Russian (read, write, speak=1)

REFERENCES

Professional and personal references provided upon request.

Stan's reverse-chronological résumé is longer than his functional résumé (about 2-1/2 pages) because it contains more details and he has three decades of professional experience. He also provided just a brief description of his duties for employers that go back 15 years or more, as much of that work was in his previous career in the Earth sciences and was not relevant to his most recent career. Depending on the industry and the type of position being applied for, such job details typically need only refer to the most recent 10 to 12 years experience.

I know for a fact that Stan customizes his résumé to address the specific duties and requirements of whatever position for which he is applying. At one point, he had five variations of his résumé circulating in the marketplace at the same time for five slightly different positions. Each version had the same layout and presentation, which was organized to help find different information blocks quickly. Take note.

Résumé Format and Presentation

There as many suggestions about résumé presentation formats and style as there are résumé writers, so your personal preference-seasoned-with-common-sense issue is the order of the day. Study the examples in this chapter and review the hundreds of examples online. Most outstanding examples follow two basic rules: (1) keep it simple, and (2) two pages or less.

If I am like most hiring managers, here is what I want in a résumé format and presentation:

- No more than two font styles (one for headings; one for body content)

77

- White copier or printer bond #24 or #28 paper
- Common fonts and font sizes (Times New Roman, Palatino, or similar; Arial, Helvetica or similar—no Courier or exotic fonts; 12 or 14 point on headings with 10 to 12 point size in body content)
- Conservative use of bold and italics (use bold to highlight quantifiable achievements, such as percent improvements, dollars earned/saved/costs avoided)
- Vertically aligned bullet lists (bullet lists help the hiring manager find information quickly)
- No spelling errors; perfect punctuation (more than 75% of hiring managers reject applicant résumés with spelling errors or grammatical mistakes, according to the *Society for Human Resource Management*)
- Generous use of white space (at least 1" margins all the way around the edges; additional spacing between information blocks to show separate content areas); white space is a design element, so consider its use appropriately

How About a Video Résumé?

That sounds like a creative and unique way to be remembered by hiring managers, right? Well, before you pull out the video camera, have you ever heard of Aleksey Vayner? As a senior at Yale, he created a video résumé entitled "Impossible is Nothing" for potential investment banker hiring managers, and he never dreamed of the results. He included video clips of his weightlifting expertise, some dance moves that would make Baryshnikov blush, and his own unique diatribe about the ingredients for attaining success in the working world. One of those hiring managers emailed the video to his friends, and from there it went to *YouTube*, where it instantly went viral.

The media and bloggers everywhere ran with the story, thereby making Mr. Vayner's humiliation total and complete. You might still be able to watch the video at *YouTube* (it is disappearing fast off the Internet being replaced by parodies) and review the *Wikipedia* and *Google* entries to read the press (most of it bad) he continues to generate. A wild and crazy guy, for sure.

Besides the video résumé just being an ineffective medium for getting a hiring manager's attention, Mr. Vayner mistakenly believed that a résumé was about *him*, and not what his skills, knowledge, and experience could do for the hiring manager. I think the grammatically incorrect title of the video résumé should have been a clue (or a warning).

A Final Word

This chapter covered a lot of information about résumés, but there is more in *Appendix B: Résumé and Cover Letter Checklist*. Do not (e)mail a résumé or cover letter without first running it through all the elements in *Appendix B* or using the free cover letter assessment at www.jtkirk-author.com.

A good *PSKE Portfolio* should include both types of résumés and whenever you update one, you should update the other to avoid having to rush to get one completed at some future date. Being able to place one version or the other in the mail *today* rather than *tomorrow* after you have updated it could mean the difference between getting called for an interview and missing out altogether.

Chapter 5
Cover Letters: Selling the Sizzle

THE COVER LETTER IS YOUR INTRODUCTION to the hiring manager, and recalling that you have just seven seconds to get his or her attention, you want to make such an impact that they proceed to (1) read the rest of the cover letter, (2) feel sufficiently motivated to read your résumé, and (3) schedule you for a phone screen and/or in-person interview. Nothing less than that should be acceptable.

How do you do that? Well, you will not do that using neon-colored paper, off-beat, wacky fonts and font sizes that look like the top or bottom line of an eye chart. You keep it professional in tone and style, but with a marketing/promotional slant that serves as a "brochure" of sorts. It advances you as a proven solutions provider and problem solver the hiring manager needs.

The best way to understand the writing tone of a cover letter that is an attention-grabber is to look at examples of good and bad cover letters.

This first cover letter is an example of way too much information from a candidate for an editor-writer position at a professional association. The substance of the letter is all over the map, and that map does not include directions to how this candidate meets the requirements for the advertised position.

Cover Letter Example 1: Poor Example

Dear Hiring Partner:

An unrelenting drive and an uncanny ability to tell stories on behalf of those who cannot tell it themselves, is what sets me apart not only as a writer but as a human being. I have been intrigued with communication since an early age. While I am seeking a more demanding career change, that thirst has not diminished. I thirst that I believe can benefit your firm.

While I have received a number of writing accolades, I find that the most fulfilling achievement that I could get is a sincere "Thank You." Years ago I did a 5-part series on child abuse. I examined the effects of physical, emotional and sexual abuse whether performed by strangers or those closest to us. And a week after the series was published I got a call from a prominent politician who thanked me for my 20work. He also confided in me that he was a victim of sexual abuse as a child and my work deeply touched him. And that feeling that I got at that moment was worth more than any plaque or decorative award.

My ideal place of employer would offer a clean, creative, relaxed yet businesslike environment. I require little to supervision and work best without someone standing over me. As my own harshest critic I find this produces my best work.

At first glance I may seem subdued and demure, but I use that time to access my surroundings. And as professional as I am, I find that people like to talk to me and easily tell their stories and thoughts. Through cooperation I find I can easily make things happen. In the global society that we live in no one can afford to be an island. But like anyone else there is a not so amiable side.

During deadlines I'm not always the best person to be around. When I feel strongly about a certain course of action I will wholly make my voice heard.

Originally from Shreveport, La I am the eldest of four brothers. While we grew up in church we are not the most religious of families. I love to do community service. Growing up in a "less than privileged" home I grew to understand how it feels to depend on the assistance of others and now how important it is to give back.

The listing for this position requested salary requirements. I am hoping to make no less than $55,000 however I would feel more comfortable negotiating this figure following an interview and further discussion. I have attached my résumé and salary requirements. Thank you for your time and I hope to hear from you soon.

Wow. Besides the poor punctuation and grammar, there are several examples of inappropriate content for this cover letter. I have little doubt the hiring manager who read this cover letter rejected this candidate without looking seriously at the accompanying résumé. Here are a few issues with this cover letter (highlighted in gray).

- *Dear Hiring Partner*: Impersonal salutation just does not cut it. A simple phone call is all it would take to obtain the name of the hiring manager or the individual screening résumés.
- *I thirst*: an obvious typo that should have been caught.
- *5-part*: preferred use is "five-part"
- *20work*: an obvious typo that should have been caught. Many hiring managers will reject a candidate for typos on cover letters and more so on résumés.
- *employer*: should have been "employment."

83

- *little to*: omitted the word, "no" after "to".
- *access*: should have been "assess".
- *La*: abbreviation for Louisiana is "LA".
- *...not the most religious of families:* what does that have to do with the open editor position?
- *and salary requirements*: this person stated his salary requirements earlier in the paragraph, so no need to repeat that he has included it with the résumé.
- *Thank you for...*: no need to thank someone for reading the cover letter—it is their job; big mistake to "hope to hear" from someone—especially if you do not have a name to recognize when and if they call. Tell the hiring manager when *you* will call *him or her* to "further discuss how I can add value in this position to your organization" or something to that effect.

It is obvious this individual failed to proofread the cover letter—or even have a good strategy for getting someone to look at his/her résumé. Do not make the same mistake. Read and reread the cover letter in a quiet setting, then ask someone else to read it because the mind sometimes has a way of tricking the author's eye to see what *should* be on the printed page, not what is actually there.

Another big problem with the cover letter is that it did not address the needs of the organization as stated in the job posting—there was just too much *I/me/my* in the letter.

Apparently, this candidate wanted to impress others more than he/she wanted to get hired for the available position.

Here are some important statistics to keep in mind as you write your cover letter:

- Instances of the word "I": 29
- Instances of the word "me/my": 10
- Instances of the word "you/your": 4 (this number should be greater than the others)

Focusing too much on I/me/my rarely will get a hiring manager's attention; as a hiring manager, I want you to tell me how *you* understand what I need in a candidate and the expectations of the position for which you are interested. Trying to sell me on how great *you* are does not work; selling me on how great you can make *my* team, *my* product line, *my* division, or *my* company definitely gets my interest.

This next cover letter comes from my friend Stan Smith (you saw his résumés in the previous chapter) who I helped coach through a job change with the cover letter and résumé redesign for available technical communications manager positions within the same industry. Stan has received three interviews based on the strength of his cover letter alone (so he was told by the hiring managers who interviewed him). Take note of how he focuses on the needs of the hiring manager and the organization by quantifying his accomplishments with other companies within the same industry. Others have had success with getting interviews using Stan's cover letter model.

Cover Letter Example 2: An Excellent Example

Dear Mr. Jones:

Do you think your company would want a **Technical Communications professional** who has

- Led an organization-wide information development initiative for establishing a database publishing effort that resulted in **an estimated $2,600,000 savings in publishing costs over 3 years**
- Designed and co-developed a training database that allowed technical professionals to better plan training and career development that resulted in **a savings of $75,000 annually**
- Developed/managed a process that provided simultaneous content for hardcopy, CDROM, and Web sites that resulted in a **66 percent efficiency improvement to the documentation development process**
- Designed and developed documentation templates for engineering teams that reduced the product-spec-to-user-manual effort that resulted in a **20 percent process efficiency improvement**
- Managed the ISO 9000 Level II and Level III documentation effort for a process control/ industrial automation company that resulted in an **ISO 9000 registration on the first attempt,** and
- Designed proposal development processes and written proposals that **have generated $50 million in contract and joint-venture awards.**

Those are just a few examples of what I can do for your company. It's always an advantage to have an **Information Design and Development professional** available to help your software information projects transfer knowledge to customers. But what if you don't have that value-add resource to lead your technical communications efforts? You call me: **Stan Smith.**

My résumé details **twenty-five plus years providing publications project management and information design and development** services and products to a variety of clients and employers in many different fields, where I have specialized in supporting many initiatives, including:

- System-level software and hardware documentation releases
- "Bleeding-edge" microprocessor support documentation
- Organization-wide database publishing initiative (Web- and SGML-based)
- Euro-bug initiative (European Union Year 2000 Metrics Standards)
- Y2K initiative
- Multimillion-dollar oil and gas exploration programs
- Data warehouse initiative
- Managed electronic commerce initiative that optimizes and guarantees round-trip e-commerce transactions

Besides managing teams of technical communications professionals, I have authored or coordinated the development of hundreds of user manuals, reference manuals, tutorials, product briefs, data sheets, data books, CD-ROMs, engineering bulletins, errata, proposals...you name it, from soup to nuts, I've been involved with it.

I have a proven twenty-year track record of continually adding value to the projects for which I was responsible. I can do the same for your company. I will call you in a few days to discuss how I can help you be more successful in an increasingly competitive marketplace.

The first thing to note in Stan's cover letter is how he begins with a rhetorical question: "Do you think your company would want a Technical Communications professional who has..."After reading the bulleted and highlighted, quantified accomplishments (in dollars or percent efficiency improvement), the obvious answer is "Yes!" and he does it within the seven-second attention-grab window. Those kinds of achievements stand out and Stan made sure hiring managers would see them by using a bold typeface.

I asked Stan what his secret was for being able to quantify the dollar and percentage amounts for those projects he worked on. He said the key was to keep a project journal and keep it current with how well the results matched the initial goals and objectives. With internal company projects, the numbers are always something that is reported to upper management so retrieving financial or statistical information on many projects is not difficult. He adds:

> *While my job title may be "technical communications manager" or "information development manager" I see myself more as a problem solver for the people on my team, the various stakeholders within the organization with whom I work, and to our customers. That means wearing many hats at different times, but to promote myself internally and externally in the marketplace as that problem solver, I have to be able to show how I helped resolve the larger issues, and usually dollar figures or statistics show that best...and I may need those numbers when I need to justify a raise or promotion request, or as supportive information for an annual review.*

Notice the promotional tone to Stan's cover letter, especially in the second paragraph ("you call me: Stan Smith") and the last paragraph. In the last paragraph of Stan's cover letter he does not "hope" to hear from the hiring manager—he is *going to call* the hiring manager in a few days to discuss how he can help the organization "be more successful in an increasingly competitive marketplace." Even if Stan fails to speak with the hiring manager, he has raised his visibility a notch by making the phone call and either leaving a voice mail message or leaving a message with an administrative assistant. Stan's letter exudes confidence as well as the sense of urgency and ownership that hiring managers like to see.

I also know that those bullet points in Stan's cover letter come from his résumé. They represent the key quantified results of his skills, knowledge, and experience, and provide a very good indicator of what he is capable of achieving in the future with another company. Stan knows his résumé and cover letter inside out and they provide him with many of the necessary talking points that he uses in interviews.

Here are Stan's numbers for his cover letter:

- Instances of the word "I": 8
- Instances of the word "me/my": 2
- Instances of the word "you/your": 11

The cover letter model is one I use over and over again for people in many industries. It focuses on addressing the issues of concern to the hiring manager instead of a first-person narrative touting any self-perceived greatness of its author.

Next up is another cover letter I received for a senior technical writer/editor position at a microprocessor design company. Writing and editing microprocessor design documentation requires special skills and knowledge that differ somewhat from writing and editing software documentation. This particular job posting cited specifically that individuals without the requisite experience (seven years documenting microprocessor design and architecture specifications) and minimal education requirements (bachelor's degree) would not be considered, yet the unqualified résumés came flooding into the office.

Cover Letter Example 3: Good and Bad Mix

Dear Mr. Kirk:

Please consider me for the senior technical writer/editor position advertised at www.jobsintown.org. Having spent the past 3+ years documenting Advanced Energy power supplies and mass flow controllers used extensively on tools in semiconductor fabs, I am very experienced with the front end of chip manufacture. As a semiconductor industry technical writer, I have dealt extensively with complex specifications, sliding deadlines, and the high-pressure gray area between R&D and manufacturing. Hard-won experience has taught me how to balance what has to be done with what I'd like to have done.

I am an enthusiastic technophile, and a long-time fan of Company X products. I have extensive DSP and microprocessor architecture familiarity, and I get along excellently with highly-technical scientific and engineering types. I thrive in technical environments, and I would revel in the opportunity to work with the premier chip manufacturer in the world. My enthusiasm for the subject matter, coupled with my confident, professional demeanor, make me a highly-desirable technical writer candidate. Perhaps most importantly, my experience in the field has taught me how to get things done in a large corporate environment.

Additionally, I have experience documenting very complex firmware and software products for a variety of end-users, and then delivering these products in an assortment of hardcopy and online formats. I have project management experience, as well as extensive user and task analysis expertise. I have a Master's degree in writing, and I have taught composition and advanced rhetoric at the college level for several years.

My editing skills are superior and my knowledge of writing for different purposes and audiences well-developed.

Last, I have six years of US Navy electronic technician on-the-job training. Not only has this experience developed a robust knowledge of electronic science, it has taught me how to perform with grace under pressure.

You need someone who can "hit the ground running" for this position. I am that writer. I am expert at FrameMaker, Acrobat, and Visio. I have semiconductor industry documentation experience, and my standards are high while I am able to deliver my products on time, every time. I am a quick learner, and I enjoy working in a fast-paced and technical environment that requires I use my multi-tasking abilities. I love to learn new technology, and I enjoy the challenge of staying on top of a fast-moving R&D schedule. But perhaps most important, I am an excellent team player who is courteous of others.

In short, I would be delighted with the opportunity to interview for this position at Company X. And once you meet me, I believe you will want me on your team.

Sincerely,

This particular cover letter has a mix of good (self-promotion tone) and not-so-good elements:

- *Please consider me for the technical writer/editor position*: Never lead with a plea as it reeks of desperation. Not a good start to the cover letter.
- *enthusiastic technophile*: Can you go to jail for that?
- *long-time fan*: "Dedicated sycophant" was not a requirement for the position.
- *highly-technical*: adverb-adjective phrases usually are not hyphenated—might sound too "picky" but it is not a good sign for a candidate for a technical editor position.

- *make*: subject-verb disagreement—should be "makes."
- *highly-desirable*: I would expect to read "highly desirable" in a dime-store novel, not in a cover letter.
- *very complex firmware and software products for a variety of end users*: the job posting did not request candidates with this expertise.
- *variety of end-users*: the microprocessors (and documentation) we designed and produced were used not by "a variety of" end users, but by engineers who use those devices in other products. *Their* customers are end-users. "End-user" documentation often means a writing style that avoids technical language, which is not the case with microprocessor architecture and design specifications. Not what we were looking for.
- *user and task analysis expertise*: Usually associated with understanding how users perform certain tasks; here, it refers to structuring documentation to accommodate how users proceed through learning and using software; a good skill to have in general for a technical writer, but it was not what we asked for.
- *Knowledge of writing for different purposes and audiences (well-developed):* Similar to the "variety of end users" statement; a good skill to have for the different types of end-user documentation and audiences associated with software products, but again, it was not part of the posted requirements.

- *Six years of US Navy electronic technician on-the-job training*: For me, this was a plus—a technical writer/editor with a hands-on background in electronics. However, HR established that the minimum requirement was a bachelor's degree in the physical sciences or engineering, so it effectively ruled out this candidate from any further consideration.
- *Love*: Uh...avoid the word "love" in a cover letter unless it is your last name or that of the hiring manager.
- *R&D*: Research and development: it was not part of the posted job description or experience requirement.

Here are the cover letter statistics.
- Instances of the word "I": 26
- Instances of the word "me/mine": 15
- Instances of the word "you/ yours": 4

OK, I could go on with more issues in this cover letter, but I am going to cut this guy a break. All of the items listed worked against this candidate to varying degrees. The two biggest: (1) no bachelor's degree, and (2) the cover letter did not fully address the requirements and experience needed for the position—it focused more on his accomplishments without tying them into the needs of the team.

Here, then, are the things to remember when constructing an effective cover letter:
- Personal salutation is a must.

- Quantify your accomplishments with dollars saved/earned or percent improvements whenever possible. If you do not have that information, start collecting it now.
- Use bulleted lists and highlight (in bold) those major accomplishments to draw attention to them.
- Avoid a narrative writing style (it is self-serving and more difficult to read than bulleted lists).
- Avoid pleas to be considered for the position—even if you have been out of work for several months.
- Avoid sounding like a sycophant (a person who tries to please someone to gain a personal advantage).
- Be confident and assertive in the tone of your writing.
- Address the requirements of the job posting in the cover letter (preferably in the quantified accomplishment bullet list).
- Close the letter by stating when you will follow up with a phone call and follow through within a few days—and make the call!
- Proofread your final draft carefully and run spell-check before putting in the (e)mail.
- Keep it short—one page or less.

Run Your Name Through Search Engines

If you have written articles for newsletters, industry-journals, or websites, or presented at conferences and had those presentations published in a *Proceedings*, it is easy to see how far your words have radiated out into various communities. Enter your name in any search engine and review the hits that the search engine matches. Do not be surprised to see how far and wide your work may have traveled. It is further evidence of your being perceived as an expert in that field.

Don has an impressive publications list with more than 80 industry articles in the earth and space sciences, marketing, and communications. Here is what he has to say about using Google to enhance his *PSKE Portfolio*.

> *In 2003, I wrote an article on how to design a template for software requirements specifications, known as an SRS, which is a key document for understanding a customer or client's needs for a software project. The article was very well received by the readers of the initial publication; however, several years later I discovered that my article is referenced by Wikiversity, The University of Bellarat in Australia, Eastern Mediterranean University's Computer Engineering Department, Bucknell University Computer Sciences Department, and the Environmental Protection Agency Office of Enterprise Technology and Innovation Publication OETI-PMP-07. I still occasionally receive emails from people with specific questions about SRSs, even though I haven't worked on an SRS in more than six years.*

A Final Word

It is impossible to evaluate cover letters for every type of position and industry here. What I can show you are the elements of cover letters that will get the attention of hiring managers and improve your chances of getting your résumé reviewed and possibly being called for an interview (be sure to review *Appendix B: Résumé and Cover Letter Checklist*).

The hiring manager's time is a valuable commodity and you must keep that in mind as you put together your strategy and structure your *PSKE Portfolio*. Cover letters should focus on how your expertise meets the requirements of the posted position and written from the perspective of how you understand the hiring manager's needs and priorities (not a regurgitation of what you have accomplished over the years—I can read that on your résumé—if I get that far).

You have to see and promote yourself as the solver of other people's problems. Hiring managers and HR managers assemble a job offer for you because you are a potential profit center, either directly or indirectly, so speak to that need.

Your employability is closely correlated with your ability to solve problems for others, and that skill and knowledge is what carries you from one job or career to the next. The portability of such expertise goes far in both good and not-so-good employment environments.

Chapter 6
Supplemental Documentation: Give Them Something to Remember You By

I COMPETED IN SPEECH CONTESTS when I was a member of Toastmasters International. Speech contestants (usually five) drew numbers to determine speaking order in the contests. Everyone wanted the No. 5 slot because as the last speaker, the odds were better for getting a higher score as there was a belief that judges had a tendency to remember speaker No. 5 better than speaker No. 1, and that judges scores tended to higher later in the competition. Sure enough, more often than not, Speakers 3, 4, or 5 came out on top. Speakers No. 1 and 2 had to have *very* memorable speeches to emerge victorious.

As a candidate for a job vacancy, you are in a similar position, and the same principle about "speaking order" and judges applies: interviewers tend to remember the last one or two candidates better than the first few. So, since you can not schedule your slot with other interview candidates and you do not know (usually) whether you are the first or last on the candidate interview list, what can you do to increase your odds of being "memorable"? Do what sales people have been doing for decades: use leave-behind items.

Sales people use brochures, demos on CD, product data sheets, and other similar information products designed to leave a lasting impression with a potential buyer. You should do the same: create marketing tools as giveaways to enhance your chances of being "memorable."

Here is a list of some of the leave-behinds I and others have used (by themselves or in combination):

- Bibliography of published articles with your contact information at the top of each page
- Detailed list of patent awards with your contact information at the top of every page
- Copies of a recent industry article or conference paper
- CD-ROM or portable USB drive containing all of the above

Chapter 4 shows examples of patent awards and a short bibliography of published articles, so let us take a closer look at the last two items in this list.

Copies of Recent Industry Article or Conference Paper

If you present conference or symposium papers, include a copy of your latest one in your *PSKE Portfolio*. The same goes for articles you have had published in industry magazines or refereed (peer-reviewed) professional journals. Such publications go far to help establish your credentials as an expert in your field.

Some companies pay employees publication awards for presenting papers or talks at conferences and symposia. Such talks and publications enhance corporate visibility, share innovative product development or process improvements, and elevate the perceived value of the company image.

I participated in a publications award program at a former employer. The awards varied from $400 to $1200 per conference paper, and if a presentation was involved in addition to the publication of the paper in a *Proceedings* volume, an additional $100 was paid out per presentation. At one international conference held in Orlando, Florida, I gave four presentations ($400 each), participated in a panel discussion ($100), and had all four papers published ($100 each) in the *Proceedings*. My publication award for that conference totaled $2,100.

While many such publications awards programs may have been scaled back or eliminated entirely recently, nevertheless, publication does offer other payoffs: perceived expertise, enhanced reputation, and the title of "published author."

You should have at least one or two samples to your credit if you are a senior-level professional. Being a published author provides a great sense of accomplishment and pride, not to mention the perception it creates and credibility it establishes as your being an expert. If you have not yet written articles about the products, skills, or knowledge your profession requires, make the commitment now to begin doing so. In today's highly competitive environment, you need every advantage available to help differentiate you from other outstanding professionals looking for work. Being perceived by interviewers as an expert in your field is such a powerful hook for you as a candidate because companies like to hire the best in the field.

I once interviewed for a contract position with a large international company where my manager-to-be worked at a location in another state. We conducted several phone interviews and during the first interview, he said he felt he had known me for several years, even though we had never met in person. He had read my articles in various industry publications and journals, and had heard me present at a conference, followed my participation in online discussion groups, so I had already established my credibility with him before I had my first interview. In his mind, the contract (which later turned in to a great full-time position I had for six years) was already a done deal—signing the job offer paperwork was just a formality.

CD or USB Drive Containing Résumé, Bibliography, Writing Samples

The CD or USB stick just consolidates the other pieces of information into one medium. Keep the samples brief and germane to the position—you just want to provide a concise overview of your skills. If you include your latest one or two creative works, ensure they have some relevance to the position, product development, or industry for which you are interviewing.

Provide leave-behinds with each person with whom you interviewed if more than one function was represented (operations, manufacturing, and marketing, for example); otherwise one set should suffice for an interview team within a single function. Before you leave the interview, get the business cards of all who participated. Whether you were the first or last of many interview candidates, your name will stay at the top of the list by sending a note thanking them for their time in helping you understand the requirements of the position and the opportunity to share with them your qualifications for the position. And let them know you are looking forward to (not "hope to be") working with them soon.

As a member of the interview team and a hiring manager, I can tell you this extra touch does work—especially if all other considerations are equal—to place you in a great position to get an offer of employment.

The Ultimate Leave-Behind Piece: "How <Your Name> Contributes to the Strategic Objectives of <Company Name>"

What follows is a generic version of one type of leave-behind piece I have used with much success over the years.

Modify it and add to it as necessary for your own purposes, but keep it to one page.

1. I can fill in gaps in thinking to help customers use your products.
2. I can transform the raw ideas into communication that transfers knowledge to customers.
3. I can transform disorganized information into a consistent message for customers.
4. I have an excellent facility with language skills and apply them to all projects.
5. I have an understanding of the variables and factors that affect communication.
6. I stay current with practices, tools, technology, and research in my field.
7. I know and use more than one method for reaching customer audiences.
8. I am a customer advocate, consultant, and advisor, with the customer's success in mind.
9. I use project management techniques on all major projects.
10. I am an expert in my <field/profession/specialty>, which means I can do it quicker and right the first time.
11. I am a generalist who juggles many concurrent projects; I can also be a focused specialist as the need dictates.
12. I work hard to grasp technical concepts and view the product/service from the customer's perspective.

13. I am the subject matter expert in my field in a variety of applications, methodologies, and tools.
14. I have the skills, experience, and knowledge to add value to any company project.
15. I can find flaws in content or ambiguity in arguments and find the means to resolve them.

What Your PSKE Portfolio™ Should Look Like

Your *PSKE Portfolio* (the collection of documents) represents not only your past professional accomplishments; it also heralds your capability to solve problems and add value to future projects.

Your portfolio should contain the following documents (that you know backwards and forwards) when you arrive for an interview:

- Reverse chronological résumé (more than one copy for the interview team)
- Functional résumé (more than one copy for the interview team; you will use one or the other type of résumé, but it is a good idea to have both current)
- Lists of references (ensure you have first received approval from individuals you list as references)
- Bibliography of publications, if you have more than six or eight
- Detailed patent descriptions, if you have any

CONFESSIONS OF A HIRING MANAGER

- Copies of your latest article, white paper, industry journal article (as long as it is relevant to the job)
- Any press coverage you received as a result of your work or your service
- A CD or portable USB drive containing as many of the above items (in PDF format so they can be read across different computer platforms) with a nicely designed label that has your contact information on it
- Any "leave-behind" item that helps reinforce your name and your expertise in the minds of the interview team

Place these items in a briefcase or portfolio with divided compartments to complete the professional image you want to convey. Never show up to an interview with paperwork stuck in a manila file folder. It does not present the most professional look nor does it paint you as an organized, take-charge individual.

A Final Word

Hiring managers have discovered a new twist on "supplemental documentation" that they are using as a tool to evaluate potential job candidates. I have already placed a shot across the bow about removing questionable content from blogs, social network websites, and other easily accessible locations. Even if you do not provide links to such sites, a query with any search engine may provide the information that you did not, so not placing links to such sites does not prevent a hiring manager from seeking your virtual presence out on them.

Now that being said, you can use blogs, forums, and social networking sites to say something profound, insightful, or just plain useful—something that a potential hiring manager would deem as a positive use of such technology and a way to supplement whatever documentation you leave with the interview team.

Here are some guidelines to keep in mind for leaving digital footprints that will not embarrass you or stifle your job chances:

- Select the "networking" option for your reason for joining *Facebook, MySpace,* etc. Avoid the "dating" or "friendship" option as that in itself may suggest something about you that does not sit well with a hiring manager (too many online dating stories end up as *Movies of the Week* starring Meredith Baxter Burney).

- Make the commitment now moving forward that you will add only positive, insightful, enlightening posts— especially if your pages are already polluted with negative images or postings; make the content useful.

- Avoid joining questionable forums that could throw doubt on your character, motives, ethics, and common sense—the "I only joined to do research for a book" excuse has already been used by *The Who* guitarist Pete Townsend and that did not win him any new fans.

- If you have a common first and last name, then you may have to keep a vigil for any inappropriate postings by others who happen to share your name. Should that be the case, you may have to alert others that no, you are not "THAT Amy Winehouse."

The key takeaway in this brief chapter is to understand the requirements of the position for which you are applying. The order of supplemental information on a résumé is important only as it relates to the specific duties for that position, and not about which information blocks you think have more importance or which ones sound impressive. It is about which ones the hiring manager will deem more critical—because it is always about the hiring manager's needs.

Chapter 7
Getting the Job: How to Control the Interview

CONGRATULATIONS! YOU HAVE A JOB INTERVIEW! You evidently sold the prospective hiring manager in your cover letter on your accomplishments and capabilities, and your résumé was of a caliber that demanded it be placed on the short list. Now the real work begins. You have generated interest with your cover letter, added momentum with your résumé, now it is time to close the deal in person. As a hiring manager, I have far too often seen candidates who looked great on paper, but who completely let opportunity slip through their grasp during the interview.

A job interview is an exchange of sorts—a give-and-take exercise where the company finds out about you in more detail, and you discover (actively rather than passively) other aspects of the position for which you are interviewing. You must prepare for both exchanges if you want to leave a lasting impression, while being aware that interviewing is on one level a game of psychology.

107

One key element of getting a job is being able to control the job interview. Many books and articles teach you to "prepare for the interview" but often from a defensive posture. This advice seems to be more of an exercise in anticipation than purposeful information gathering on your part. This approach prepares you emotionally and mentally for being the person under the microscope, which naturally raises nervousness and stress levels. In this chapter, you will learn how to prepare for job interviews from a proactive, politely assertive position. After all, you are interviewing the company to see if what they offer is in line with your own abilities, expectations, and career goals.

The strategies, tactics, and tips in this chapter are the actual ones I have used in the past to obtain interviews for the following positions:

- Manager of Information and Proposal Development for an eCommerce software company (accepted)
- Technical Publications Project Manager for a large semiconductor/microprocessor manufacturer (accepted)
- Manager of Worldwide Technical Media for a mid-size microprocessor manufacturing company (declined)
- Several contracts (as an independent contractor)

Research the Company

The first step in preparing for your interview is to know your résumé backwards and forwards; the second step is to conduct research on the company with whom you will be interviewing. Company information is easily available through

- Corporate websites
- Annual reports
- Business journal articles
- Newspaper articles
- People you know who work there
- Search on <company name> on *Google*

Get some idea for the corporate culture, the work environment, the products or services offered, the benefits package (check out *Fortune* magazine's "The 100 Best Companies to Work For" annual issue), the financials (in light of Enron, Arthur Andersen, WorldCom, and Bear Stearns, by all means, check out the financial stability and what corporate ethics programs the company offers employees), the prognosis for business growth, and any propensity for rounds of layoffs in the recent past (some companies have an unwritten "last in, first out" downsizing practice).

Make special note of any items for which you would like more information during the interview, and be sure to mention the source, as in "I noticed in your annual report that...." Or "I read in *The Wall Street Journal* that your company..." This tactic reveals two things about you: first, your inquisitiveness shows that you are someone who has a genuine interest in the position and wants more information before making a decision; and second, you do your research. You have answered two of their questions just by asking one of your own or making a statement.

Prepare for Your Interview Questions: Prepare Your Responses to Anticipated Questions

While this step may seem like you are being asked to develop ESP, it really goes to preparing your responses to questions you already have a good idea will be asked. The "anticipating questions" is the defensive strategy; the "preparing responses" is your offensive strategy.

As a hiring manager, I view your cover letter as a calling card, which, if done right, further interests me in what you have to offer in the way of expertise I have a need for. If your résumé interests me even more, I will call you for an interview, because I am hiring *you*, not your résumé.

All skills, knowledge, and experience being equal among candidates, most of the time I will hire the one that makes an impression on me on a professional and personal level. In other words, if you present yourself as a likeable person during the interview, people will be interested in what you have to offer. However, if we do not connect on a personal level—regardless of your skill set—it will be difficult to get an offer from me or any other hiring manager. Someone once told me "people don't care how much you know until they know how much you care." Establishing rapport and a positive connection is what opens doors for others to see and hear to what you have to offer. If there is no connection or you appear to be "high maintenance", well—sorry, there simply is no room for that on the team (there is no "I" in "team").

Write down those questions and your responses, but keep this in mind when you do: every one of your verbal responses should be constructed in such a way that conveys to interviewers that you are the complete professional they have been looking for. Your apparent extemporaneous answers to the open-ended questions from the interviewing team are really prepared responses you anticipated. Facing the interview team in a conference room is not the time to be searching for answers. You may look good on paper, but if you have difficulty articulating responses to interview questions, you drastically reduce your chances of getting hired, especially for senior-level positions.

When I interview candidates, I pay attention to how well they communicate their responses to my questions as well as their questions to me about the available position. Candidates who have to search for answers or look around at the walls while they respond (or inquire) create the perception that they are not well prepared. I can tell you this: during interviews with job candidates, many hiring managers think beyond the immediate position to: "does this person have what it takes for a leadership position on the team or department? Will this candidate be assertive enough to get the tough answers and solutions needed to perform his or her job? Am I getting the 'real deal' like the résumé says?"

Nothing Prepares Better than Preparation

Over my career, I have been involved with public speaking, starting with the high school debate and extemporaneous speaking team. I was involved with Toastmasters International for 10 years and the National Speakers Association, have taught at the university level, presented seminars and technical papers at conferences across several industries. The big secret to being an effective speaker, presenter, or instructor is *preparation*, no matter the circumstances in which you find yourself. When you are thoroughly versed in your materials—whether that material is the information on your résumé or new advances in a technical area—responses to questions flow more eloquently and in a logical manner. You are better able to maintain eye contact with interviewers, giving off an air of confidence and self-assurance instead of looking around at the floor like you are searching for lost change, or glancing at the ceiling as though counting holes in the tiles.

Here are a few questions you can count on being asked at some point in your job interview journey through the years. These questions demand prepared responses in advance:

1. *What are the 3 or 4 best things your coworkers and manager would say about you?* (*Correct responses*: any response that demonstrates (1) your *sense of urgency* to all project work you undertake; (2) your sense of *ownership* in all project work you undertake; (3) your *demonstrated professionalism* in all that you undertake,

and for 10 bonus points (4) as a value-add service provider, your *ability to facilitate the success of others.* (Yes, you can use those terms in your response.) These concerns form the kernel—the core criteria—of what hiring managers are looking for in a candidate beyond the requisite skills and knowledge needed for the position.

2. *What is the worst thing your coworkers and manager would say about you?/What is your worst quality?* (*Correct response:* any response that balances a negative with a positive, such as: "I seem to do my best project work when I have multiple priorities to manage. When the project workloads back off, I look for ways to improve the process..." (**Note:** be careful here and remember to offer a balanced response. Most hiring managers are wise to the "I work too hard..." response.)

3. *Describe a no-win situation or project you found yourself in and describe how you handled it.* Make sure you have already mapped out a response that demonstrates your problem-solving abilities as well as how you addressed your "best" traits mentioned in Question 1. Always try to tie in a response that addresses one or more of these areas: (1) sense of project urgency; (2) sense of project ownership; (3) demonstrated professionalism; (4) being a facilitator for the success of others, which can be the team, the company, the customer.

4. *How do you handle competing multiple project priorities?* *Good response:* any response that demonstrates your ability to (1) manage client expectations; (2) negotiate priorities with others ; (3) arrive at win-win solutions all the way around. One response:

> *I've learned in my experience that there's no such thing as "multiple priorities"—only negotiated priorities. I have found that when I am approached with a new project that competes with existing projects underway, the solution usually involves a tradeoff of other priorities that are sensitive to internal client and external customer expectations so that a win-win solution is the result.*

Another good response:

> *I always say "yes" to new project requests, but when projects or schedules collide, I ask: "what must I remove from the existing list of projects to finish them?" That's how priorities get negotiated.*

5. *In your opinion, what is the purpose of the <function for which you are interviewing>?* Ultimately, whatever response you provide addresses one of more of these concerns: (1) "I see me in this position as a key contributor to the company's bottom line success by <increasing revenues, avoiding unnecessary costs, etc...>; (2) "I see me in this position as a <facilitator of

customer satisfaction and success with company products/services...>.

Here are four categories with sample questions in each you can expect at some point along the interview process. Not all of these categories will apply to the particular position for which you are interviewing, but over your entire career, you probably will hear most of them.

General Questions

- Tell us about your most recent work experience (focus on accomplishments, achievements—not tasks, duties)
- Why did you leave your last job?
- Please explain the employment gaps in your résumé
- How do you see this position and why are you the best qualified candidate for it?
- What satisfied you the most about your last job?
- What frustrated you the most about your last job?
- How would you rate your knowledge or skill level with <specific tool, process, software, methodology, policy>?

Behavioral Questions

- Describe a situation where you had to...
- Describe a time when you had to...
- Describe a difficult problem you had to solve...
- Describe a project where you had to...
- How do you deal with difficult people who...

- Describe an instance when you had to circumvent company rules to complete a job...
- Describe any incident where you had a disagreement with a peer or manager and how you handled it...

Customer Support Questions

- How would your last manager portray your relationship with coworkers?
- Describe a customer support issue that you resolved to the satisfaction of the customer (can be internal customer or external customer)
- How do you prioritize competing priority requests?
- Describe how you manage multiple stakeholders with competing priorities on a customer support issue?

Miscellaneous

- Why should <company name> hire you?
- Do you have any questions for me/us? (You should be asking a few questions throughout the process to show your interest)
- (Actual interview questions I had to field) Why is a carrot more orange than an orange? How do you get a two-ton elephant into the freezer? (designed to elicit a creative response as there were no wrong answers here)

Bottom line: you must use every opportunity during the interview to not just answer the questions from interviewers, but *provide them with the answer you want them to walk away with.* In other words, answer the question, but couch your response in a manner that incorporates one of the core criteria mentioned in Question 1. That involves planning ahead and taking a more assertive versus defensive approach to the entire interview process.

How to Control the Interview Process

That sounds like a bold claim, I know, so let me explain how this works. This point bears repeating: everything you say during an interview must pertain to establishing yourself to the interview team as the complete value-add solution provider this company is looking for. In a manner of speaking, you can not afford to be yourself completely at an interview; however, the interview team must get a feel for how well your personality might mesh with others on the team or with any other functions, and how you might fit in to the corporate culture.

Most people who are asked to interview a job candidate are not trained in interview techniques, so "help" them by initiating conversation that does two things: (1) makes you approachable, and (2) opens the door for you to sell yourself using your résumé as selling points. Here are some other ideas:

- Ask them to tell you about their job and the work they do ("Can you tell me about what you do here...")
- Ask them how their work might interface with the work required of the available position ("Can you describe

how the work you do might be tied to the duties for the available position...")

- Ask them about the standard software, hardware, tools they use on the job ("What software/hardware /tools do you use for your everyday work...")

- Turn your résumé into topics of conversation ("I see that the company has achieved ISO 9000 registration. I have experience working with the ISO 9000 audit process...")

- Ask them if they have any questions for you

There is a fine balance here between offering too much and just enough information. For example, if asked: "Do you like sports?" a just-enough response would be, "Oh sure. I love baseball and college football." A too-much response might be to add to that first response with: "...but I hate professional football—everyone's a 'bad boy' or 'gangsta' wannabe." Could be the hiring manager has a son who plays for the Chicago Bears. While you may be technically qualified for the position, you may have just made yourself a "bad fit" for the company. Keep your responses focused and pertinent to the position for which you are interviewing. Be sure that your responses to informal conversation do not ignite any controversy.

Your objective after leaving the interview is for the hiring manager and interview team to want to know more about you. Companies want to hire candidates who can present a positive image for the corporation and who make a favorable first impression, which is critical for all positions, not just sales and marketing. Making a positive first impression helps foster cooperation between and among teams and different functions inside and outside of the company.

Here is a short list of personal information that is appropriate, borderline, and inappropriate, respectively, for interviews:

Appropriate Personal Information to Share

- Goals and aspirations – where do you want to be in 5 or 10 years?
- Professional growth – highlight training and education you have had for professional development.
- Achievement highlights – relate the most rewarding professional achievements without exaggerating or bragging.
- Inspirations/motivations – what excites you about your profession, the positions you held in the past; what is it that gets you up in the morning (besides the obvious need to meet a mortgage payment).

Borderline Personal Information to Share

- Vacations – stay away from how you spend lengthy vacations unless it has a tie-in to a corporate interest.
- Pets – exotic pets may be perceived as potential problems (tigers, boas, cockatoos, tarantula farms, etc.).

119

- Extreme sports/hobbies – "I enjoy outdoor activities" is a much better response to such questions instead of "rock climbing, cliff diving, rugby, participating in X-Games..." You do not want to be perceived as someone who may require lots of sick leave/extended leave to "mend" from such outdoor activities.

Inappropriate Personal Information to Share

- Lifestyle/religious/political preferences.
- Health history – you want to be perceived as a dependable, reliable individual. That perception a prospective employer has of you includes your general health from your appearance; you must position yourself in the most favorable light in the eyes of the prospective employer.
- Family plans – do not discuss your desire to be the next Octo-Mom, or the 57 cats you take care of in the spare bedroom.
- Other personal information – stay away from discussing previous bad bosses, out-of-control teenage Twitterers, how long your spouse has been out of rehab for the second time, car problems, etc.

You may encounter a member of the interview team who goes off in the weeds with questions that do not pertain to the duties of the position for which you are interviewing. No need to panic—just take the initiative (take control) to bring them back to the focus of the discussion: your qualifications for the position.

I was interviewing for a very visible manager position at a medium-size international company. The position (in technical communications) reported to the vice-president of corporate communications. I was scheduled to interview with three different people in an hour. One of the interviewers was an engineer who worked at the same company I used to. Judging by his questions, he had no idea about the responsibilities and duties of the position for which I was interviewing.

He began asking me engineering questions to test my knowledge of microprocessor design and electrical engineering. After several minutes of this fruitless approach to the interview, I decided to take control: "Excuse me, but if I brought in all my engineering reference books, I could easily look up the answers for you, but I'm interviewing for a non-engineering position and, with all due respect, this line of questioning doesn't seem to address the responsibilities of the position for which I am interviewing."

I then proceeded to explain my understanding of those responsibilities and how my experience, skills, and knowledge would be used to meet them. I asked him about how I (in this position) might help him with his job, should I receive a job offer. I used his remaining 15 minutes as a platform for promoting myself as the value-add solutions provider (stop me if you have heard that phrase before) his company needed. That was a big risk, but his approach would not have resulted in a fair assessment of my capabilities for the position.

When you prepare yourself mentally to take the initiative in the interview process, you find that taking such risks is easily justified. After all, the only person looking out for you is *you*. The risk was also mitigated more by the fact that I was already working for another company when I was being interviewed by this company. Such a situation improves your bargaining position because typically a larger compensation package (salary, benefits, stock options, vacation time, etc.) may be necessary to entice you from your current position at another company than it would if you were not employed.

As a result of my taking control of that portion of the interview, I later learned he gave me the highest recommendation of the interviewers. The other two interviewers did not have any better understanding of the responsibilities of the position either, and so I repeated my performance with each of them.

I did receive an offer from this company but my questions during the interview with the vice-president gave me concern that the budget I would have to work with would be nowhere near what I would need to hire the team for the duties of the position. The economy was beginning its downward slide in 2001 and I had some anxiety about making a move from my established position with another company. About six months after I rejected the position and offer, that company reduced their workforce by 20 percent.

Answer Questions with an Unforgettable Response

When the interviewing process gets past the small-talk stage, invoke your strategy of answering questions with a response you want the interviewers to remember after the interview is over. When an opportunity presents itself for you to wax eloquent, do not be shy, but keep the self-superlatives to a minimum; just give them the facts. Give them direct eye contact and say: "Yes, I do have experience working on database publishing initiatives. In fact, I co-chaired an eight-month effort at a former employer that involved benchmarking our company's efforts with that of a competitor, where we actually shared methodologies with each other. The result of our work demonstrated that we could save $2.3 million in publishing costs over three years." How would you know that so well? That tidbit is on your résumé.

Or, you could have responded with: "Yes, I've worked on database publishing initiatives before." From the hiring manager's perspective, which is the more memorable response? Which one does a better job of putting you on the hiring manager's short list?

This is where being the author of articles or conference papers helps establish you as an expert. If you wrote an article or conference paper on how you helped save your organization $75,000 a year in training costs by developing a training evaluation database, such information (which should be on your résumé) can be brought out as a response to a question,

123

such as "Have you ever worked in any capacity with the development of training materials or coursework?" Seal the deal by handing the hiring manager a copy of that article or conference paper.

In fact, many if not most of your responses may sound like you are repeating that information on your résumé (with the appropriate elaboration during the interview). And what is wrong with that? *Nothing*; you are using the information about your professional expertise to your advantage in an interview. Interviewers have looked at so many résumés that they probably do not notice that your responses come from your résumé that is sitting in front of them. Your résumé becomes your study guide, your script for the interview. For each bulleted accomplishment on your résumé, think of two or three different questions that might be asked that could be answered with that bulleted item as a lead-in response.

Preparing Your Samples: Think "Minimalism"

You may be interviewing for a position that could require samples of your work (written, audio, video, programming, visual, demos, etc.). If you have been asked to bring in samples of your work, bring with you only those samples that demonstrate your abilities for the type of position and project work you might be involved with. Busy people will appreciate your showing them pertinent samples; nothing more, nothing less. Stay focused.

Explain the extent of your involvement with the creation of the sample. If you designed a product, say so; if you were involved with storyboarding a video, but not the actual final production, say so. That way, the interview team has a better understanding of your capabilities, not to mention the fact that claiming someone else's work as your own is dishonest; such *plagiarism* and can have legal consequences. If someone on the interview team knows you did not write/design/build/create something for which you are claiming, you could be branded a liar and a thief. Not a good career move.

If you have written many industry-related articles or columns, bring along a few copies of a bibliography of those articles—*just in case* someone asks because they noted it from your résumé that a publications list was "available upon request." The same can be said for a copy of your most recent (but pertinent) article.

One caution: do not bring a sample you can not afford to leave with the interviewers. If you have an original work or a master you sweated over for months, make a copy. Consider uploading it to your personal web site (if you have one) or placing it on a CD or DVD you can leave with the interview team. See *Chapter 6, Supplemental Documentation* for details.

Interview Mistakes You Must Avoid

The number of people who continue to remain clueless about the interview process still never ceases to amaze me. I have heard everything from noisy parrots to toilet flushes in the background during phone screens of potential interview candidates—I have even had a candidate arrive for an interview with alcohol on his breath at 8am. That brand of mouthwash definitely worked against him. Such people obviously fail to convey a positive first impression, which is something a successful candidate would never allow to happen.

In its annual survey of the worst interview mistakes, *CareerBuilder* reports these gems:

- A candidate answered her cell phone and asked the interviewer to leave her own office because it was a "private" conversation
- A candidate told an interviewer he would not be able to stay with the job very long because he thought he might get an inheritance if his uncle died, and his uncle was not "looking too good"
- A candidate asked the interviewer for a ride home after the interview
- A candidate smelled his armpits on the way to the interview room
- A candidate said she could not provide a writing sample because all of her writing had been for the CIA and it was "classified"
- When the candidate was offered food before the interview, he declined stating he did not want to line his

stomach with grease before going out drinking with friends

- A candidate said she was a "people person" and not a "numbers person"—in her interview for an accounting position
- During a phone screen interview, the candidate flushed the toilet while talking to the hiring manager (I see I was not the only one to experience this behavior)

According to a *CareerBuilder.com* annual survey of hiring managers, the biggest mistake made by candidates during interviews is not dressing appropriately. Now, "appropriately" can mean different things to different people and involves several factors, such as the normal workday dress code for the particular industry/profession in which you want to work, the particular job function/position, and the geographic region of the country (or world) where you live or will work/live. The dress code for a Wall Street banking firm in Manhattan will be different than the dress code for a gaming software startup on Sixth Street in Austin, Texas, or an oilfield roughneck on the North Slope of Alaska. Even a Linux programmer will put on his good sneakers if he has to interface with customers (probably not a good idea, though—the Linux programmer meeting customers, I mean—not the good sneakers).

So the advice for dressing appropriately for job interviews is to know the workplace and interview culture for your geographic area, for your industry, and for your anticipated position in an organization. When in doubt, dress up a notch.

A close second on the *CareerBuilder.com* list was badmouthing a former boss. Such behavior immediately pegs you as a "sour grapes" employee, willing to throw others under the bus to further your own cause. Most everyone has had at least one bad boss, so just accept the fact that you are or will be a member of the club and let it go because it is the professional thing to do. Remember your mother's advice: If you can not say anything nice about someone, do not say anything at all.

Third on the list was appearing disinterested during the interview process. I have interviewed highly qualified candidates whose nervousness came across to other members of the interview team as being "disinterested." Your interview "game face" should convey confidence and interest in the position and its attendant work as well as an interest in the people with whom you will be interviewing.

Fourth and fifth on the list were being arrogant and not providing sufficient responses to interview questions, respectively.

Sealing the Deal

The interview is your chance to sell *you* to the hiring manager and the interview team on what you can do them going forward. That means translating your past accomplishments into future potential for prospective employers. By now, you should know your résumé inside and out; understand how you will respond to interview questions, keeping the four criteria in mind with every response; and having leave-behinds for the interview team to help them remember you out of the field of interview candidates.

I also suggest practicing your interview technique with someone acting as the interviewer. Practice everything from your handshake, eye contact, interest level, and ability to answer questions with responses that leave a memorable impression with the interviewer.

Abraham Lincoln once wrote that if he had just six hours to chop down a tree, he would spend the first hour sharpening his axe. Prepare for both the obvious and for the contingencies that may arise, and you will have done all that you can to ensure a successful job interview.

"But What if I Don't Get the Job?"

If a job offer does not materialize after an interview for which you have fully prepared, take heart: you are one interview closer to getting that job or career you want. Another way to look at the situation is *not* that you did not get the job—the hiring manager and interview team failed to recognize the value you could have brought to the company (I like that spin). "Ultimately, it's their loss" is a positive way to accept the experience because it does not diminish you or your capabilities at all. And when you finally land that great job where the

129

company and you are a perfect fit, all the failed interviews will eventually fade from memory. Who knows—with people changing jobs or companies an average of seven times over a career, you still might end up working for the people who turned you down earlier. It happens all the time, and particularly so in the high-technology sector.

Tom is an engineer with whom I have worked over 15 years and three companies together. He was once a manager for a division engineering team at Company A. He left Company A for greener pastures at a small engineering startup. Soon after, Company B bought the division in Company A. The small startup is now struggling to keep its doors open and lights on. So, Tom just got hired by Company B (after once not getting the job for which he interviewed) for a key engineering but non-managerial position. He is working with many of the same people he used to manage, but is now a peer of theirs. He was highly regarded as an engineer and manager, and the engineering team was very happy to have him return.

A Final Word

Two former workshop attendees have this to say about how they prepared for their interviews.

Tina S, Santa Clara, CA

> *...I kept a detailed log of how I prepared for that interview and my impressions of the interview afterward. Other factors that helped my case were the*

recommendations from the department chairman as well as from the cooperative education chairman from my school. Application forms leveled the playing field, but the clincher, I was told, was how I sold myself in my introductory letter and interview.

Paul F, New York, NY

...Over time, I have crafted the elements of my PSKE Portfolio and interviewing technique that have garnered many high-paying and personally rewarding positions in the telecommunications field. The number of interviews increased once I understood that my chances for getting the job I wanted were better if I simply embraced the attitude that I was filling a need within an organization and packaging myself during interviews as the best "need filler" available.

Treat the interview as a chance to sell the hiring manager and interview team on <Your Name Here> Inc. The documents in your *PSKE Portfolio* serve as a platform to promote you as the complete professional who is best qualified to fulfill the requirements of the position—because everyone else is just looking for a job.

Chapter 8
Negotiating Your Compensation Package

IN NEARLY ALL CIRCUMSTANCES WHERE PEOPLE work together, they arrive at agreement in ways that sometimes short-change the interests of all parties involved. Typical negotiation strategies often leave people stressed, angry, and further entrenched in their initial position. Just look at labor union negotiations with management; sports agent negotiations with team owners; lawyers negotiating with other lawyers. All too often, negotiations deteriorate into pitting personality against personality.

Principled negotiation takes a win-win approach to concession and compromise without involving posturing or personalities. A successful negotiation is simply arriving at a compensation package that makes both you and your new employer satisfied that you each got what you wanted out of the process.

"Negotiation" or Concession and Compromise?

Unlike most kinds of business negotiations that involve give and take from both or all parties, the process here involves additional concessions on the prospective employer's part without any expectation of the same from the successful job candidate. Therefore, my use of the term "negotiation" really addresses the process of fine-tuning the salary and/or total compensation package for a candidate.

Many job candidates who have successfully navigated the screening and interview portions of the hiring process fail to realize that a few elements of a proposed compensation package a prospective employer offers are negotiable. For many critical positions, HR personnel often consider the job offer a starting point for negotiations though most people simply accept the first offer they receive. The compensation package you are offered may be "standard" for most non-executive employees in the organization, but just because it is the standard package does not mean you can not ask for—and often get—some "options" (figuratively and maybe literally).

Salary and benefits are based on several factors, including local/regional competitive salary and benefits for the position or type of work, the general condition of the economy (are businesses expanding or are they waiting for better times?), and how well the specific business does in the marketplace (local only, national, international), to name a few.

Most of the time, the numbers that go into the equation that yield a job offer are considered the minimum compensation necessary to get you to accept the job and keep you on the job (so says an HR manager friend). It is not about how much your skills, knowledge, and experience are worth by themselves but in relation to what the salary and benefits folks think the market can bear. In many professions across a multitude of industries, you do have *some* negotiating room nonetheless—but there is a strategy for doing so that improves your chances for success.

What Most Candidates Do With an Offer

Most successful candidates do one of two things with a job offer from a prospective employer: they either accept it if they deem it a fair offer, or reject it if deemed not. Most fail to realize there is a third option: ask for a better deal. People often wait too late in the hiring process to begin their negotiations— usually when the ink is dry on the official documented offer that is in the mail from HR. You have to start sooner than that.

When is the Best Time to Begin a Negotiation?

Depending on the type of work, industry, and available position, you may receive a phone call or letter from HR after the interview process has completed that states your being offered the position for which you interviewed at a starting salary of $X per year. That number may make you very happy, or you can respond with a counter offer.

In other cases, the time to start negotiating for a better compensation package is *after* all the interviews are completed, when someone first asks: "So, what are your salary requirements?" It is a mistake to respond to that question during the interview process because the number you toss out may take you out of the running for the position before the interview is over. You want to be considered for the skills, knowledge, and experience you can bring to the job, and not disqualified based on a salary figure.

But before you utter any type of response to that question, you must have mapped out your strategy for this important part of the hiring process. You must also understand the factors that influence your probability of success before thinking about negotiating a better compensation package:

- More senior-level and/or executive-level candidates will have better odds at successfully negotiating an improved compensation package.
- Depending on the industry or field, technical candidates may have better chances of negotiating a compensation package than non-technical candidates; in others, marketing and sales positions may have more leverage with negotiating compensation packages.
- Candidates with unique or highly sought-after skills, experience, education, or knowledge will be more

successful negotiating compensation packages than those without them.

- Recent college graduates, people out in the job market for the first time, or those returning to the job market after being away for some time (ex-military, stay-at-home parent, etc.) generally will have little to no room for negotiating a compensation package.

- The candidate with excellent communication skills and just the right amount of unabashed self-promotion has a better chance of a successful negotiation than those candidates who do not possess them.

A total "compensation package" can include any combination of these elements: salary, paid vacation, paid sick time, health/medical/dental/vision insurance, education reimbursement, company car, flex-time, work-at-home policy, performance bonus, expense account, stock options, restricted stock units (RSU), 401K, pension plan, employee stock ownership plan (ESOP), maternity/paternity leave, employee retail discounts, subsidized lunches or snacks, subsidized gym/health club memberships, and much more.

Not everyone is interested in a larger salary; some candidates may want to negotiate for an extra week of vacation or not have to wait six months before they are eligible for any vacation; some may want another five days of paid sick leave, or a waiver of restrictions on the number of work-at-home days allowed per month. Different candidates will have priorities for which they may want to negotiate.

The hiring manager who has authority to "tweak" a few details of a job offer must still have those tweaks approved by HR and maybe even upper management, depending on the size of the company and position.

The "Give and Take"

The most important "offer tuning" technique I have taught others is a very simple one, and that is to answer a question with a question. When most candidates are faced with the question: "So, what are your salary requirements?" they blurt out a number, and many times, that number has not been well thought out. The danger is that *your* number might be much lower than *their* number, and you have therefore, "left money on the table" that could have been part of your salary or total compensation.

As a hiring manager, I have used that technique many times on candidates because part of my job was to hire the most qualified candidate for the position at the lowest possible *competitive* salary possible. I have never—nor would I ever—give a "low-ball" offer to a candidate. I have simply offered a number (from HR) that represented a combination of local competitive salary figures for the duties of the position, the education level of the applicant, and other factors. I would expect a candidate—a sharp candidate at that—to know when he or she possesses hard-to-find skills, knowledge, or experience, and to know that such expertise is worth a premium in salary or other perks—and ask for it. I have also gone to HR to ask for more money for a deserving candidate as well.

Do not expect a hiring manager or HR representative to build in to an offer any "consideration" for highly specialized skills or knowledge you may have. While the offer might include *some* consideration, use your unique skill or knowledge as a negotiating point to bump up the salary or other options in your compensation.

Negotiating for a better compensation package begins with knowing in advance what it is you want and need in the way of salary, insurance, vacation, retirement plans, etc. and working with the hiring manager and HR to accomplish those goals.

Salary Negotiation Example

Open-ended questions about salary requirements for candidates usually result in their leaving money on the table. While you may have a salary number in mind, there is no harm in trying to discover how close or far apart their number is from yours. For example, consider these three hypothetical scenarios that focus on the salary portion of the compensation package:

Scenario 1: (Salary information states "competitive")

Hiring Manager: "So, Jim...we'd like to extend an offer to you for the position. What are your salary requirements?"

Candidate Jim: "Well, uh...I 'm looking at $62,000..."

Hiring Manager: "Great, Jim...I think we can accommodate that number...how soon can you start?"

Scenario 2: (Salary information states "competitive" in ad)

Hiring Manager: "So, Jim...we'd like to extend an offer to you for the position. What are your salary requirements?"

Candidate Jim (*his ballpark number is $62,000*): "That's great news...what is the salary range for the position?"

Hiring Manager (*continuing his non-committal position*): "I can tell you the range is very competitive for the position..."

Candidate Jim: "I know that's what the job ad states. What exactly would that range be?"

Hiring Manager (*realizing he must provide more information*): "It's a senior level position, as you know, and the salary range is from $59,000 to $67,500."

Candidate Jim (*seeing he initially underestimated his value*): "Well, based on what I can bring to the position, I believe the upper end of that range is close to my salary requirements."

Hiring Manager: "So, $67,500 is what you need?"

Candidate Jim (*asking for more than he needs to be able to settle on what he wants*): "Actually, $69,000 is the number I need to move forward."

Hiring Manager: "Hmmm...that's a little out of the range for the position...let me see what HR has to say...

(Later in a phone call) Hiring Manager: "Jim, the absolute best we can do for you is $68,250..."

Candidate Jim: "I think that's a fair offer, and that's acceptable. I can start in two weeks, if that's agreeable."

Scenario 3: (Salary of the position has been posted in the ad)

Hiring Manager: "So, Jim...we'd like to extend an offer to you for the position. Do you have any questions?"

Candidate Jim: "Well, I'd like to know if the posted salary of $63,500 for the position can be adjusted...I'm very interested in being a part of the team but the posted salary doesn't quite meet my requirements..."

Hiring Manager: "What are your salary requirements, Jim?"

Candidate Jim (*not wanting to kill the deal by blurting out a number*): "Can you tell me what the salary range is for this position?"

Hiring Manager: "It's a very competitive range..."

Candidate Jim: "So, the posted number represents a midpoint of the range...low-end...?"

Hiring Manager: "Pretty close to mid-point, yes..."

Candidate Jim: "Well, given my expertise, I feel that a salary of $68,250 is more in line with what I can bring to the team..."

And the negotiation continues from there. Candidate Jim may not get the $68,250 figure, but there is a good chance he will get more than $63,500.

Because Candidate Jim responded to the hiring manager's questions with more questions of his own and stated his case (based on his proven ability as a solutions provider) for a higher starting salary, he got it. Without that strategy, he would have left $8,250 on the table. Scenario 2 is based on an actual salary negotiation session I coached someone through recently.

These very simple examples illustrate that you often need more information before you can make an intelligent decision about certain components of the compensation package—the salary in particular. Do not allow others to pressure you for a salary figure without asking legitimate questions first so you can make an informed decision. Control the negotiations.

Benefit Negotiation

Many candidates prefer to negotiate more flexible benefits than direct salary, and most companies are willing to participate. The most popular negotiated benefits are flex-time schedules, work-at-home options, and vacation time. Sometimes these negotiations are temporary and involve agreements with hiring managers without the involvement of HR; others—particularly long-term changes—may require approval all the way up the management ladder.

If they had to, many candidates would be willing to accept a lower salary in exchange for working from home two days a week, or not having to wait six or twelve months to be eligible for vacation. Others would prefer to negotiate a flexible schedule where they can take their kids to school or pick them up after school during the week. Many employers will yield to such requests *without* a candidate having to surrender salary levels. The employer may set up boundary conditions for the special consideration, but generally, if the work is being completed on time without any sacrifice to quality or schedules, such requests often are granted.

Some positions provide stock options (non-qualified stock options, or NQSOs), where you are granted a number of shares of company stock at a reduced purchase price that vest (ownership transfers to you) at different periods in the future. Some companies also provide restricted stock units (RSUs), which are actual shares granted to you that you can sell at some future date. For some employees, particularly in high-growth (and high-risk) technology companies, stock options and RSUs have been the carrot used to entice qualified applicants to come onboard (though options have lost their initial luster over the past few years).

Many companies provide for education reimbursement (so long as the course or degree work is related to the job) and many folks consider that a primary motivator rather than a top salary. If participating in professional association meetings and attending conferences is important to you, such opportunities for professional growth should be an agreeable negotiating term for most employers because you both benefit.

A Final Word

Do not become too mired in the term "negotiation" because it really fails to capture the essence of what transpires in discussions among the candidate, a hiring manager, and HR. The process is more of a personalization of the elements that constitute the complete compensation package than any *bona fide* concession exercise with a "winner" and "loser."

Only within the last 15 years have companies embraced flex time, working from home, child-care and elder-care subsidies, fitness club membership subsidies, dry-cleaning valet service, and flexible medical spending accounts (called "cafeteria options") as standard benefits for employees. You do not have to trade a lower salary for such benefits (or most benefits for that matter); they may already be part of your compensation package. Just ask.

The secret to controlling salary and compensation discussions is to continue asking questions so you have more information with which to make an informed decision. You may be able to ask for more than you need in order to settle on exactly what you want—but you need to know where the initial package boundaries are drawn first so you know how far to extend them for your circumstances.

Chapter 9
Other Options: Temporary Work and Independent Contracting

A BOOK ON DEVELOPING STRATEGIES for changing jobs, getting a job, or changing careers would not be complete without a chapter on contingent plans of action that run parallel with your primary objective. Keeping in mind that it is much easier (financially and emotionally) to find another job when you already have one, the idea of temporary work or contracting work is a wise approach to your overall goal, but even finding temporary work may not be easy these days.

According to *OfficialWire.com*, temporary employment in the U.S. declined by 76,000 jobs in January 2009, the 24th monthly reduction in temporary jobs over the last 25 months. The decline of 22.7% on a year-over-year basis was the largest decline since 1990. But the U.S. Bureau of Labor Statistics reports that from April-July 2009, that drop has leveled off. As of July 2009, 8.8 million people work part time for economic reasons (sometimes known as involuntary part-time workers).

Most folks have heard of temporary work and understand how it works, but may not be aware of the pros and cons.

Temporary Work Defined

Temporary employment is a work arrangement where a worker is hired to work for a specified time period, which can be anywhere from a week to a few months. Work that is seasonal in nature uses temporary workers. Outside of agricultural areas, most temporary workers are hired by an agency ("temp agency") that specializes in providing workers for a particular industry or profession (health care, accounting, and administrative are three major segments). The agencies place these workers in client companies, though many companies can hire temporary workers directly. Temporary employment can involve part-time or full-time work, though the benefits provided to temporary workers are usually far less generous than those for permanent employees.

Pros and Cons of Temporary Employment through an Agency

- *Less competition*: People who meet technical requirements for the type of work are often virtually guaranteed a job without the more involved selection process used for permanent hires.

- *Lower pay*: Temp workers make on average 33 percent less than permanent employees; most businesses that use temp workers are in low-paying hourly-wage sectors.

- *Flexible work hours*: Depending on the type of work, temp workers often are offered a choice of which shifts to work; the ability to take time off (often without pay) for weekends, holidays, vacations (usually after six months or a year of work), personal appointments, or for any other reason of choice, or to work on such days for additional pay. They can choose to work part-time to devote their efforts to looking for the job and career they want.

- *Instability*: They work for the temp agency; the company where they perform the work is the temp agency's client, so the client has no real commitment to the temp worker much beyond the day's need. However, the consequences for getting fired from a position within a client company or simply finishing up a project or contracted work period are lower than for permanent positions. But as an employee of the temp agency, the worker can be placed in similar open positions at other companies if they are available.

- *Little or no benefits*: Many temp agencies offer only minimal benefits. Shop around to find the agency (or agencies) with the best overall package for your needs.

147

Benefits packages comprise 30 to 40 percent of a permanent employee's base income.

- *Little accountability*: Temp workers often work in environments that offer minimal accountability due to the short-term nature of the work. Less accountability often means lower stress levels, too.

- *Variety of tasks and duties*: Temp workers often tackle a variety of tasks and projects that help keep boredom to minimal levels, but realize that many times, temps do the work that full-time permanent employees do not want to do.

- *Weekly payday*: Unlike full-time permanent co-workers who likely get paid every two weeks, many temp workers draw a weekly paycheck.

- *Outsider Syndrome*: Temp workers usually are not included in various team meetings or department activities, which over time can lead to the feeling of always being the "outsider" – a "stranger in a familiar land" as one temporary worker told me.

- *First indicator of resurgence in hiring across the board*: an increase in the number of temp workers is the first sign that hiring across the board may be on the increase.

The biggest advantage of temp work? It places you in a work environment. OK, so you are not doing the exact kind of work you would like or you are not making the kind of money you need, but you are around people who may take notice of your initiative, your sense of project urgency, your sense of project ownership—no matter how menial the task—and decide to offer you a full-time position with full benefits and higher salary. You never know—a coworker in the workplace might know someone who is hiring in a different department or at another company.

Many companies also offer "temp-to-permanent" employment if the temporary assignment works out to the benefit of both you and the temp agency client. Keep an eye out for that type of arrangement if you are starting out in the workforce because it is a great opportunity to get not only on-the-job experience, but hopefully to get an employer to provide training opportunities or reimburse higher education expenses if they provide that benefit once you are hired as a permanent employee.

"Temping" is exactly what it is made out to be: temporary employment, and accepting temporary employment means you understand some compromises and sacrifices will have to be made on your part *for the interim*. You have to look at temporary employment as a stepping stone in your strategy to secure the job or career you want, and not some dead-end time waster.

But Will Temp Work Hurt My Career Objectives Later?

Many folks looking for a job or a career change are concerned that any temp work on their résumé may hurt their chances for getting hired at competitive salary levels they had in previous positions prior to layoffs. The vast majority of employers recognize that many people have had to accept work and salaries far below "norms" when folks were working in their technical or professional specialty. Having temp work on a résumé should not have any significant effect on interviewing or hiring decisions made by prospective employers.

Independent Contracting

Given the current state of the economy, workers with an entrepreneurial spirit and many employers have created more opportunities for independent contractors than ever before. Independent contracting can be another avenue for you to pursue as part of your strategy to find the job and career you want.

If you are the type of person who needs routine working conditions that are predictable and planned, then independent contracting may not be for you. But if you have an adventurous, entrepreneurial spirit that embraces new challenges, then working as an independent contractor might offer you the excitement and opportunities you want.

Independent contractors are sometimes called *ICs*, *consultants*, *freelancers*, *free agents*, and just *contractors*. Regardless, all are self-employed for tax reasons in the U.S. where earnings are reported on IRS Form 1099 versus the standard W-2 for employees.

Contracting work is usually longer in duration than temporary work, pays a higher hourly rate, and often involves more autonomy as to how and when specific work is to be completed. If someone provides direction how a task is to be performed or how a project is to be completed, you are either a temp worker or an employee. Contractors are often brought in to help on projects where little or no direction is needed to complete the job. Companies hire your services, not you.

For example, when I hired technical writing contractors, I did not have to teach them grammar or technical writing skills, nor did I have to teach them how to use the software applications that are common across the industry for creating technical documentation. They needed minimal training to understand how to use documentation databases where files were stored for editing, but beyond that, they knew what had to be done and by what date.

Just as there are temp agencies that hire out temporary workers, there are contracting agencies that hire out contractors (software programmers often work through contracting agencies, for example, and likely receive W-2s from the agency), but many prefer to work as independent contractors where they make a higher wage because they have to pay for their own retirement and health-care benefits as well as self-employment taxes. Independent contractors also can take more business deductions for expenses than can employees.

In many industries and companies, contractors are not allowed to participate in internal meetings or other initiatives open to permanent employees. A big part of the justification behind this policy is to protect proprietary information or processes that the contractor may be working with (even though many companies require contractors to sign a non-disclosure agreement prior to any work).

Sometimes, preventing contractors from participating in company quality initiatives or company-sponsored programs is not such a good idea. For example, contractors who were responsible for writing software documentation for a large technology company in Dallas were not allowed to participate in the Total Quality Management training program the company sponsored. It appeared that the people who would benefit the most from such a program would be those workers creating the very documentation that customers would be interacting with. Sometimes it is difficult to be a contractor with a conscience because company policies may prevent you from doing the very best job possible.

Pros and Cons of Independent Contracting

- *Job insecurity:* Like temp workers, independent contractors do not have the same job security as employees. Independent contractors are often the first to be laid off in economic slowdowns and because they are self-employed, they are not eligible for unemployment benefits.

- *Fewer perqs and benefits*: Independent contractors do not receive the same perqs and benefits as do employees. They have to continue to pay themselves for sick leave, vacation, fund their own retirement accounts, and purchase their own health and life insurance at higher rates than what employers pay for each employee (group rates)

- *Tax responsibility*: Independent contractors are responsible for paying federal and state income taxes (where applicable) as well as self-employment taxes—on a quarterly basis, all of which requires discipline to set aside this money that does not belong to you. Commit to setting aside this money (in an interest-bearing account) first so you are not caught short each quarter. Uncle Sam does not take such lapses lightly.

- *You provide your own "tools"*: To be compliant with government guidelines regarding the independent contractor relationship, you will likely have to provide your own tools for the work you will be contracting to perform. There are many exceptions, such as in high-tech companies that may provide computers and software for contractor use, but you should understand the expectations for providing tools for your particular industry, skill, or trade. If you are fortunate to be able to work from home as a contractor, you will need to purchase your own tools (modems, tools, network equipment, webcam, etc.)

- *Expense reimbursement:* You will have to cover travel, lodging, and meal expenses if you are required to perform work out of town. Employees can expect their employer to reimburse such expenses, but as a contractor, it has to come out of your pocket to maintain the contractor-client relationship in the eyes of the IRS. Just remember to incorporate such expenses into your quoted project fee (versus an hourly rate).

Don't Charge by the Hour—Charge by the Project

One great advantage to quoting a project fee versus an hourly rate is that with the project fee, your rate incorporates the value you add to the project. In other words, your quote incorporates the expertise you bring to the project; an hourly rate is based largely on your time—and you have only so many hours a year to work.

When I worked as an independent contractor, I quoted a copywriting project for an advertising agency for an 8-page technical brochure at $2,000. The client needed the brochure completed within seven days and could not find a copywriter who was familiar with the technical subject matter (I was, however, working with that technology).

Given the immediate need and other requirements, my client did not flinch at the $2,000 quote (he passed along the cost to his client anyway, which was a small software development company). With the materials the client provided, I was able to finish the project in eight hours, which averaged out to $250 an hour. However, the going hourly rate for copywriting and editing at the time was about $45. Eight hours x $45 an hour = $360 is what I would have earned on a straight hourly quote if I charged for my time. My specialized knowledge was the value-add I provided to the project, so I charged for the value-added knowledge instead of charging by the clock.

Whenever you can quote a project fee, do so to maximize your earnings per project. But, if you have contract work that requires an hourly rate quote, sometimes you can raise your rates as the contract nears an end.

When You Get a Client, Burrow In to Get More Contracts

The best way to minimize any downtime or expenses involved with lining up clients as one contract is ending is to find another contract *within* the current client organization. If you are performing work for Company A, first determine if other contracting opportunities within Company A are possible before seeking contracting work with Companies B through Z. You are already working inside of Company A—ask around if other teams or organizations have a need for your services and expertise—there are no marketing costs or lost time between contracts because you are already *inside*. The secret then once you do get inside, is to *drill deeper* for more opportunities.

The Best Time to Raise Your Rates

Sometimes you can raise your rates as the end of a contract approaches and the client wants to extend the contract to complete a project. That is what Kevin did with the client from hell.

Kevin, a software programming contractor in Boston, was working on a six-month contract for a state health agency that was automating medical records for satellite clinics throughout the state. Kevin encountered the usual state government red tape as well as uncooperative and difficult employees on the client's team.

As the contract end date approached, Kevin was set to take his wife on a cruise in the Bahamas before starting on another contract job, but the current project was running behind schedule and the project manager needed Kevin to stay with the project another two months. Kevin explained to the program manager his plans for the cruise, but the program manager countered with: "Name your hourly rate—any rate—and we'll agree to it." Kevin did not want to continue on this project or with the team any longer, so he effectively quoted an hourly rate that was double his normal rate, hoping the program manager would blink. He did not.

Kevin made the equivalent of four months' wages in two months—even though he told me that at times he felt like the doubled hourly rate was not worth the aggravation he had to contend with. But somehow, he managed.

Jennifer worked as a contractor after she was laid off from a job she had for three years. She spent the first few months just trying to drum up contract work, which was infrequent at first, but she was soon busy 40 hours a week, and turning down requests for her professional services.

After three years working as a contractor, Jennifer was contacted by a major electronics firm about a senior-level position on a team within the company. A hiring manager at the company kept her résumé he had received several years earlier and forwarded it to another hiring manager who had an available position. The company site was less than two miles from Jennifer's house, which kept her commute costs down. The salary was above market, and the benefits included annual cash and stock bonuses as well as a retirement plan and health insurance. Jennifer jumped at the opportunity and had a very successful five-year career with that company. Her experience there eventually opened up larger opportunities at other companies.

What About Using Professional Networking Websites?

If you have access to a computer and Internet service, you will devote many hours searching through job openings, temp agencies, or agencies that use contractors. Networking with other peers and professionals in your industry or field is a great way to stay connected to trends and tips that could prove profitable in your job search. The more popular professional networking sites are *LinkedIn, Ryze, Bing, Digg, Naymz, Reddit,* and *Spoke*. Many such sites have both free and paid versions. However, the jury is still out on whether this type of online professional relationship building has proven fruitful for the job market. Jane Copeland, in her *SEOmoz* blog compares such sites to what corporate office waiting rooms would be like if they were web pages.

Recruiters ("headhunters") comb such professional networking sites for qualified candidates in a variety of technical and professional fields, so if you decide to participate, make sure you fully complete your profile (which can be a tedious process, depending on the site) as complete profiles are the best bait for attracting corporate and independent recruiters. That said, realize that online professional networking sites suffer from a major problem that online social networking sites have: developing any kind of meaningful online relationship with others (especially those in a position to get your résumé in front of a hiring manager). But I (along with others) see two paths to overcome this potential limitation, especially with *LinkedIn*, one of the premier professional networking sites:

1. *Participate fully in the Question and Answer portion of the LinkedIn site.* Provide useful information to anyone and everyone asking a question related to your expertise. It enhances your reputation as a knowledgeable expert and provides a little more insight into who you are.

2. *Engage people on their blogs.* Related to No. 1 above is engaging people on their blogs. Many of us read blogs of topics that are of interest to us, and even comment on postings from time to time. Commenting on blogs is another way for others to get a feel for who we are beyond the information on our résumés. Avoid the urge to post pithy, offensive rants on your own blog or when you comment on others if you value your professional image and reputation when seeking a job or new career (more about blogs coming up). If you have a blog, post the link to it in your *LinkedIn* profile.

With all this online job search research you will be performing, there is the temptation to flood the e-mail inboxes of your working friends and family members with *YouTube* videos, jokes, questionable content, and chain letters. Please resist that temptation—there is just too much of that floating around *inside* company computer networks to have to contend with it coming from the *outside* and it clogs up servers. One morning while writing this chapter, one of my unemployed friends sent me 20 megabytes worth of *YouTube* videos before 10am. I finally had to place his e-mail address in my junk e-mail folder to stop the constant spam. I hope he finds a job *very* soon.

Social Networking Websites: Potential Time Wasters

I briefly mentioned this caution elsewhere, but let me expand upon it here: avoid the social networking websites, such as *Facebook* and *MySpace,* as part of your job or career search strategy. If you already have such pages, scrub them of any offensive content—language, posts, and photos. You do not want pictures from that "gone wild" weekend in Puerta Vallarta available to a hiring manager checking out the link to your *MySpace* page that you included on your résumé. People have had photos copied by "friends" and sent around the Internet (even with "friends only" security and the Search function disabled does not guarantee your information stays confidential).

My friend Mike refers to *Facebook* as "Crackbook" because of its addicting nature to post all sorts of non-sensical, non-interesting, boring content (rarely can it be called "information")—and its virtual voyeuristic nature. Be careful with the settings of your "preferences" because the same non-sensical, non-interesting, boring content is "pushed" to your page every time one of your "friends" posts something on theirs. After reading these posts and writing a few of your own, you suddenly realize that you have just wasted half a day when you could have been searching online job banks.

Another danger: your personal information could be stolen. That is exactly what happened to my *Facebook* account. Someone hacked in to my *Facebook* page, and used Instant Messaging (disguised as me) to text my friends that I was mugged in London and my passport and wallet were stolen. Could they please send "me" money so I could catch a flight home? Fortunately, all of my friends recognized the email as a hack of my *Facebook* account (the email contained profanity, and that was the giveway that the email was not from me, and most everyone knew I was not in London at the time) and notified me that my account was "compromised" long before *Facebook* administrators sent an email notification about the problem.

Thus far, the social networking sites have not proven to be that successful for people looking for jobs or folks promoting businesses, so the less time spent at these sites, the better (for now anyway).

Blogs: They Can Help You Get Recruited...or Fired

While there are many well-informed bloggers who provide insightful and thought-provoking content and commentary to readers, most blogs read like incoherent rants propped up by unsupported opinion, where facts, intelligent rhetoric, logic, and truth are in short supply.

That said, it is your right to write anything you please on a blog—within reason. Want to post an anonymous "drive-by" blog rant about someone you do not like? Go ahead, but you can no longer assume full, complete, and absolute free speech protection under the First Amendment of the Constitution.

In August 2009, a New York court forced *Google* to reveal the identity of an anonymous blogger who used her "Skanks in NYC" blog to disparage the reputation of a former model for *Vogue*. The unmasked blogger turned around and sued *Google* for $15 million for "failing to protect her right to privacy."

That lawsuit probably will not stand as there is some legal precedent in what you can and cannot say under "free speech" protection.

In 2000, Judge Stanley P. Klein, Circuit Court of Fairfax County, VA wrote:

> . . .In that the Internet provides a virtually unlimited, inexpensive and almost immediate means of communication with tens, if not hundreds, of millions of people, the dangers of its misuse cannot be ignored. The protection of the right to communicate anonymously must be balanced against the need to assure that those persons who choose to abuse the opportunities presented

by this medium can be made to answer for such transgressions...

The advice is clear: think first about the type of content you want to post on a blog: what are the long-term consequences of such content? Will it help or hinder your ability to get hired or change careers should a hiring manager come across it? Could it result in your dismissal if your blog content is less than flattering about any one individual or company—particularly the company you work for?

Digital information is like radioactive waste—it takes a long time for it to fade into the noise of the background (it can be done expensively by companies who specialize in such "digital cleansing").

And most importantly, how do such posts enhance or detract from your reputation? Putting a polish back on a tarnished reputation (on and off the Internet) takes time, so if that is something you care about, think twice before hitting the "Enter" key to upload that post.

According to a recent study by *Proofpoint*, 38 percent of large companies employ people to analyze employees' outgoing e-mail. CNN and other corporations have in-house e-investigators tracking employees' public statements on the Internet and in print media. You never know how many pairs of eyes are watching your e-mail and blog activities.

Whether you are an employee or a contractor, remember that free speech is not always free.

An Offbeat But Growing Option: Working for Free

Would you consider working for free if there was a chance of being hired? As offbeat as that sounds, it is a growing trend in 17 states across the country. With more than 500,000 new unemployment applications being filed each week, states are looking at innovative ways to stretch benefits for new and existing claims. In the state of Georgia, unemployed citizens work for up to six weeks without pay at businesses that have job openings. Started in 2003, the Georgia Works Program sponsors "auditions" for paying jobs that help people get on-the-job training and provide businesses with free labor, while the workers continue to receive unemployment benefits and weekly stipends (up to $300) for transportation, child care, and other expenses. So far, 58 percent (3,000 people) of those participating in the program have been hired at the businesses where they began working for free.

The program has saved employers $15 million in labor, hiring, and training costs while saving the state $5.3 million in benefits it would have paid to people who remained unemployed. The Georgia Works Program is not federally funded and is open to all job seekers.

One 41-year-old participant in the Georgia Works Program lost his job of 22 years in January 2009. After two months of fruitless job searches, he enrolled in the program. He got the job he auditioned for at a home health-care company in

Columbus, Georgia, and his salary of $35,000 is only $2,500 less than he was making in his last job.

The program does have its critics, however. There is the fear that the program could lead to mandatory unpaid work for unemployed people should it be adopted by other states. But people already enrolled in these programs would likely disagree with the critics—the unpaid work serves as free training that allows them to get more than a job. They regain their dignity, self-worth, and self-esteem in addition to a paycheck.

A Final Word

About eight years ago, a contracting agency in my town posted open contract positions for technical editors who were skilled in various foreign languages to edit/proofread translated documents. The hourly rate: $15.00. At the time, the high-tech economy was trying to pull out of a two-year nose dive; hourly rates for skilled technical communicators were way down, but $15 an hour for these skills? Who were they kidding?

This practice is often referred to as "bottom feeding." This agency was fishing for desperate people willing to jump on a contract at any rate. "But it's better than unemployment" some say, or "better than minimum wage."

The question should be: What are you willing to do to earn a living wage? What is your lowest hourly rate or salary you would accept working in your current technical or professional capacity? Are you willing to work *outside* your specific field temporarily so you can earn that living wage? (House painters in the Austin area at the time were making $30 an hour, and most of them spoke just one language, which was not English.)

The definition of "living wage" varies for each of us depending on our marital status, how many kids (or parents) we have living in the household, as well as other factors (retirement investments, college funds, health insurance, etc.). Are you willing to uproot your family to move to another city where the opportunities are more plentiful and the pay scales higher? Are you willing to work a second job to supplement your primary income? Or are you going to wait until desperation sets in and be forced to accept bottom-feeding pay rates? Unfortunately, some folks will, and even more unfortunate is the undermining of any skill or profession that occurs when such low-ball rates are offered and accepted.

What is your "job insurance" policy? Do you have a Plan B in writing ready to put into effect should the need arise? What *other* skills do you have in your personal inventory that you can fall back on if you had to?

When Stan Smith made the transition from full-time technical professional/part-time science writer to full-time technical writer (a transition that took 10 months), he worked for six months as a part-time carpenter building homes. That was his Plan B. At the time (1986), he was making $20 an hour in a depressed housing market. Unemployment paid about $225 a week then; minimum wage was $3 to $4 an hour, but his carpentry skills helped carry him through that transition period.

Take inventory of what you can do if you had to do something other than your specialty (temporarily). Avoid waiting until you are forced to accept bottom-feeding contracting rates. Believe me, dining on *Little Friskies* and *Cheez-Whiz* more than a couple of times a week will get old fast.

While most people will consider temporary work or contracting as a stop-gap strategy while they pursue full-time employment opportunities, some folks will choose those options as life-long careers in themselves. Contracting offers the ability to work as long as you want and are able; there is no need to stop working at age 62 or 65 if you do not want to.

There is no denying that working part time, full time, as a contractor, or even working for free places you in contact with many people, and networking with others is often the best way to find the next contract, the next job, or the next career.

Chapter 10
Just for Veterans: Transitioning Back to the Civilian Job Market

FOR RETURNING U.S. ARMED SERVICES PERSONNEL, finding a job today might be the toughest personal mission yet. You have dodged sniper fire, roadside bombs, temperatures that exceeded 120 degrees, and now you are facing an entirely new "hostile fire": the current U.S. job market. You have or will soon leave a very tight-knit culture and lifestyle for a return to civilian life. Add to that environment the frustration from companies not willing to consider the types of experiences, skills, and knowledge you offer for any available positions. In the job market, an "IED" can mean "insufficient experience diversity" that prevents any further consideration for a job you know you can do.

"Friendly fire" on the other hand comes in several forms: from civilians competing for the same positions; from foreign workers willing to do what you know how to do for lower wages; and in many cases, from yourself. Let's look at what you are faced with—understanding the terrain of the job market for veterans.

Refer to *Appendix A: Resources* for organizations and websites that specialize in assisting veterans transitioning to the civilian job market. Many offer very good free information so take advantage of that.

Planning an Entry Strategy into the Civilian Job Market

You have probably heard folks talk about planning your exit strategy from the military. Regardless of your length of service, there is much planning to do for that day when you depart not just your branch of service but an entire way of life. Most of the experts say to begin that process 12 to 24 months out from your discharge date.

But the mistake so many people make is that they spend 12 to 24 months planning, scheduling, arranging, and dreaming about the day they leave military service, but they do not start their civilian job transition planning until *after* their exit from the armed forces. Naturally, folks want to take time to spend with family and friends and to get acclimated to civilian life right away, but one thing you can do prior to exchanging those green fatigues for your most comfortable jeans and t-shirt is to start planning your **entry strategy** into the civilian job market long before your discharge date.

An entry strategy involves thinking about how your military service is going to transfer to a civilian career. You will be asking such questions as:

- Which industries could best benefit from my training and experience in the military?
- What kind of work am I best qualified for within those industries?
- What kind of work do I *want* to do? How well does it align with my skills, knowledge, and experience?
- Do I want to go back to school first to finish that degree or get an advanced degree?
- Will I have to move to improve my chances of getting hired in a decent-paying job? What areas of the country are less affected by the current economy than others? What is the job market like in those areas?

Such questions also fall into the "exit strategy" category, too, so you will have your work cut out for you. But this type of thinking should motivate you to start assembling the documents for your *PSKE Portfolio* before you are discharged. Imagine how much less stress you will subject yourself (and your family) to if you are prepared to respond to job postings with a well-crafted cover letter and résumé before your discharge date!

There are no guarantees, of course, because of the many political and economic variables that influence the job market, but one thing you will do is decrease the amount of time you would have been out of work had you waited until *after* your discharge to get things rolling. While other servicemen and servicewomen are looking for a job during terminal leave, you could be lining up interviews because you were prepared much earlier with your *PSKE Portfolio*.

Scouting the Terrain of the Job Market for Returning Veterans

President Obama's troop reductions in Iraq have unavoidably added to the ranks of people transitioning from one career to another. The Department of Labor reports that the unemployment rate in 2008 for veterans younger than 24 was 14.1 percent, compared to 11.6 percent for the same age group in the general population. The unpublished, non-seasonally adjusted numbers for the second quarter of 2009 indicate veterans younger than 24 had a 26.8 percent unemployment rate compared to 16.8 percent for non-veterans in the same age group.

The Veterans Administration reports that returning veterans who do find jobs earn an average of $5,736 less per year than their non-veteran counterparts, and for veterans with a college degree, that amount jumps to $9,526 less per year.

Younger veterans have expressed frustration at the military's good intentions but ineffective job placement programs because the military does not excel at translating military experience, skills, and knowledge into a format that civilian employers understand or can assign value to.

While many corporations such as Northrup Grumman, AT&T, Home Depot, and Raytheon provide special programs aimed at hiring veterans (not to mention the $2,400 tax credit such employers receive for hiring veterans), how do you differentiate yourself from the many other ex-military applicants interested in the same available positions?

If you joined the service out of high school, you probably have never had to write a résumé or go on a job interview until now, and the biggest question facing you is "how do I transform my military duties and responsibilities into valuable skills for the civilian job market?" If you are career military with a college degree and are transitioning out after 20 or more years of service, you have the same problem. The trick is to use a language for your military experience, skills, and knowledge that resonates with hiring managers in civilian job markets.

Some Encouraging News

Let me give you two items of good news. No matter what your background—civilian or military—or how well your skills, knowledge, and experience matches a posted job opening, the majority of companies fully expect it to take some time for you to get up to speed to meet the demands of the position for which you are hired. They understand you will require up-front on-the-job training and perhaps some formal classroom-style training. In fact, that is one consideration when hiring managers evaluate any potential job candidate: if I bring this person on board, how soon before they can hit the ground running, and what can I do to help facilitate that readiness?

Obviously, the sooner the better, but very few hiring managers have any expectation that by the end of the first day, first week, or even first month, you will be performing at peak levels in your new position. While some highly technical positions require more time to reach peak performance levels than others, it is a progression of assimilating new processes, methodologies, "tribal knowledge," tools, and skills that takes time for every new employee being hired.

For many if not most open job positions across all skill and experience levels, the wording of the posting is aimed at the "ideal candidate" who probably does not exist with the exact skills, knowledge, and experience levels. As I have stated previously, many of the requirements you read about in job postings are simply "filters" to eliminate less-qualified people from applying for the position.

If you exceed some of the minimum requirements of a job posting but are short in one or two areas, apply anyway. With few exceptions (education or licensing requirements, for example), most companies will bring in the best qualified candidates (i.e., the ones whose expertise *best approaches* the requirements in the posted ad) for interviews for open positions. Many companies today give preference to a veteran if his or her background is comparable to that of a non-veteran candidate.

Lose the Military Lingo to Better Your Job Chances

One of the first exercises in transforming your military experience into know-how that is in demand in the civilian job market is to translate military acronyms, abbreviations, or lingo on your résumé that no one in the civilian job market understands. You want to develop common ground with hiring managers, not alienate them by using terminology they probably do not understand. There is an urgency your cover letter and résumé must have and they must grab that hiring manager's attention within seven to ten seconds. If hiring managers do not speak or understand military slang, they are off to the next candidate's résumé in ten seconds or less. Not using language hiring managers are familiar with is an obstacle to your being considered for most any job.

"Tanks, Weapons, and Digging Ditches"

Here are a few examples of how you translate military experience into marketable civilian skills. A key component in this translation is to focus on the *functional areas* of expertise you had rather than the individual tasks involved with those responsibilities. In essence, you have to identify your specific *core competencies* and *skill sets*.

Diane Hudson Burns' article *Translating Military Experience* on the *www.job-hunt.org* website offers great advice for transitioning from the military to civilian jobs. She mentions an individual who had been in the Army for 23 years (E-9/Command Sergeant Major), and believed his job duties in the military offered little value to corporate America. He said he operated tanks and weapons, and dug ditches. This soldier suffered from what I call "career tunnel vision" because he focused on the tasks at hand, not how those tasks were simply the implementation of a higher strategy and larger operation.

However, after an in-depth discussion, Diane determined that this Command Sergeant Major possessed significant core competencies and skill sets. He directly supervised, trained, and evaluated 40 personnel, supporting over 2,000 troops in four countries, with an inventory list of 1,500 line items, and material assets valued at $65 million (including large vehicles). His functional areas of expertise included personnel management, logistics, and operations, and later, considerable responsibility for strategic planning and tactical application.

How do we get from "operating tanks and weapons, and digging ditches" to "personnel management, logistics, operations, and strategic planning"? By asking questions.

1. *What specific skills, knowledge, and experience must you have to operate, maintain, and support the number and types of tanks and weapons, and digging ditches under your responsibility?* That type of question elevates the

task-oriented work, which initially seems to have little to no civilian job market value, to the next highest category: core competencies and skill sets, which then becomes: "supervision, training, and evaluation of personnel, international support of 2,000 troops, material asset management of 1,500 line items valued at $65 million."

2. *How would you classify **those** skill sets, knowledge, and experience into practical job function categories non-military employers would understand?* Supervision, training, and evaluation of other soldiers become "Personnel Management"; international support of 2,000 troops becomes "Logistics and Operations"; material asset management of $65 million worth of government property becomes "Inventory/Asset Management." Those three functional categories can be rolled up into "Strategic Planning and Execution."

Task-Core Competency-Functional Expertise Relationship

The progression looks like this:

Tasks→Core Competency→Functional Expertise

Basically, a series of related tasks all lead to a higher level "core competency." For example, an ability to read house plans, use power and hand tools, and frame a house suggests a "carpentry" core competency. If you can read house plans, run electrical wiring through a house, and know how to use the tools for connecting wiring to outlets, fixtures, and a master circuit breaker panel, that would suggest an "electrician" core competency. As you gain more skills, knowledge, and experience in a variety of tasks, you can add to your core competencies in such a way that together they suggest a "home builder" or "general contractor" functional expertise. See **Figure 6** for a generic representation of this relationship.

Figure 6. Generic Example of the Task-Core Competency - Functional Expertise Relationship

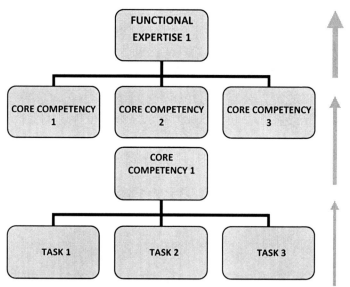

Follow this model when you begin identifying the higher order core competencies. Think in terms of how to phrase everyday tasks as part of a larger strategic operation or initiative that translates to the civilian job market.

Let's now fill in the generic blocks with tasks, core competencies, and functional expertise for **Figure 7** from the example Diane Hudson Burns mentions.

Figure 7. Specific Example of the Task-Core Competency-Functional Expertise Relationship

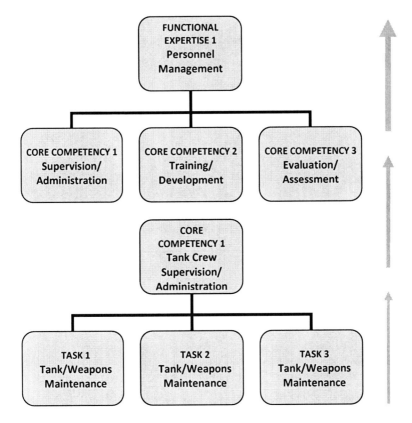

In Figure 7, I have identified just three tasks related to tank and weapons maintenance. Obviously there are many more, but the three I selected suggest a core competency in "Supervision/Administration," probably because those tasks align with providing direction to others. Other tasks (i.e., "Task 4, Task 5, Task 6" if they were on the chart) might involve an ability to explain, teach, or show others how to perform tank/weapons maintenance, suggesting a "Training/Development" core competency. These core competencies align with a functional expertise called "Personnel Management," which is an area all hiring managers in the corporate world are familiar with and would easily recognize such expertise.

Let's look at one more example.

If you worked in "Logistics Support" that required you to assist with understanding, monitoring, and improving any aspect of military operations or systems, you probably used these skills:

- *Critical Decision Making* – evaluating the costs and benefits of potential actions and selecting the most appropriate option.
- *Process Analysis and Control* – evaluating how changes in conditions, operation, and environment influence system operation and results.
- *Process Evaluation* – identifying and evaluating indicators of process performance, and actions needed to improve that performance accordingly.

A hiring manager in the process control/automation field for manufacturing would have a clear understanding of those skills. What would this look like on our chart? See **Figure 8**.

Figure 8. Logistical Support➔Process Management and Control

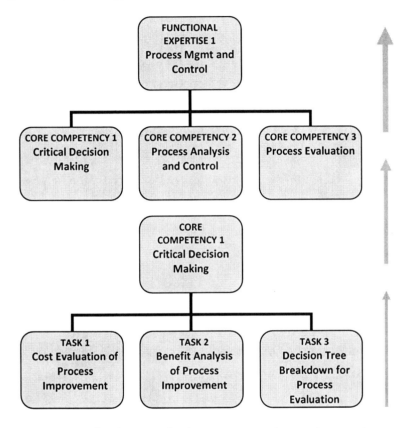

Translating Military Achievements, Awards, and Recognition

Your résumé should also include any mention of special awards, achievements, or recognition you earned while in service to the country. While you will likely not be asked to provide the official documentation for any mention of these honors during the résumé review or interview process, you should have them available and handy should a job offer be extended to you soon thereafter. The HR department will likely request copies shortly before or after your hire. In fact, if you already have official documentation in your possession, you should mention that "Official documentation is available upon request" in a sentence in the section of your résumé entitled, "Military Awards, Recognition, Honors, and Specialized Training" but before your bulleted list of such items. It shows hiring managers you are prepared to get started should you get the nod for the job. See *Appendix A: Resources* for a list of the types of official documentation you may require as proof of various military service, achievements, awards, and recognition.

Other Accomplishments

As you continue to translate your other military accomplishments, your responses to these questions may help give you the edge over others in the competitive job market:

- Have you been published in military journals, websites, or magazines? If so, where?
- Have you been quoted in those publications? If so, where?
- Have you had leadership/management training? If so, what kind?
- Do you speak at conferences or in other forums? If so, where and on what subject?

- What licenses or certificates do you hold? Are they current?
- Do you have a security clearance? If so, what level? When does it expire?
- Do you speak/read/write foreign languages? If so, what is your proficiency level in each category?
- Are you engaged in community service or volunteer positions? If so, list them.

Another Challenge: Interpersonal Work Relationships and Communication in the Civilian Work Environment

When you get hired, your transition to a civilian workplace will involve significant changes to how you approach interpersonal relationships and how you communicate with co-workers and upper management. Verbal communication in the civilian workplace ranges from informal to "business casual" and generally without any obvious or overt deference to seniority/titles (an assumed familiarity is common, such as all employees referring to the CEO by his or her first name). Therefore, you will have to be conscious of whether your demeanor and communication still has a military "edge" to it.

A peer of mine once hired a young man right out of eight years in the service. He answered every question with "good to go," "locked and loaded," "that's a five-by-five," or "negatory" instead of a simple "yes" or "no." These slang responses began to grate on this young man's co-workers to the point where the manager had to enroll him in communications training to help him adjust his communication style.

Round off those edges as soon as you can so that your assimilation into the team and company is a smooth and complete one. The most successful transitions are those where vestiges of an armed forces persona are subtle and serve you in a "silent" manner (your confidence, your focus on tasks, your attitude toward the job, your leadership and decision-making ability, your project management skills, etc.). Always be proud of your honorable service of protecting this country, but be aware that if you outwardly display too strong a military persona in a non-military atmosphere for too long, it could create difficulties for interpersonal work relationships and communication.

Larry was a new IT director for a small company in Florida. He is also a veteran of one of the military's elite covert forces. Larry never learned to tone down his former military demeanor. He quickly had on-the-job run-ins with several of the company executives, and touted the IT department as the nerve center of the company, when in fact the IT department served all other company functions. Larry's "wag the dog" approach and attitude were picked up by most of his co-workers, upper management, and subordinates. It did not settle well with people, many of whom recognized Larry's still-switched-on military demeanor. He insisted on using an automated IT support request process (a great idea for a large company), when in the past, employees simply sent emails or called the IT department (consisting of three people) for assistance. This "human interface" process worked very well for this company of 60 employees, and helped reinforce the informal, family-type work environment.

During the last company-wide employee feedback survey, Larry received the lowest rating, which was underscored by such comments as "Larry hasn't been able to turn off Commando Larry since he's been here, and he views any question or concern as a challenge to his authority or leadership...he's very difficult to work with..."; "Larry's need for control and empire building has forced my department to pursue workaround measures that bypass IT altogether—it's the only way we can get things done in a timely manner..."

After several warnings from management about his demeanor and work ethic, Larry lost his job as IT director in large part because he never learned how to fully transition from his former military communication and interpersonal demeanor to the civilian workplace. His inability or unwillingness to integrate successfully as a valuable contributor to the overall company effort resulted in his losing a very high-paying position.

Larry's situation is being repeated in companies of all sizes across the country, and perhaps for some individuals, the personal price to pay for transitioning to the civilian workplace is too great. Should that be the case, then perhaps a career in the military may be the best path for such individuals to pursue.

A Final Word

Everyone wants to see a returning soldier find a job or career, and return to a happy, productive life after having served the country with selfless honor. There are many organizations and individuals who are at the ready to help with the transition back to civilian life in many areas; few are more critical than being assimilated back into the civilian job market for rewarding careers.

Translating specialized military skills, knowledge, and experience into marketable skills for the civilian marketplace will require hard work, rework, and creativity. The same can be said for adopting behaviors typical of the civilian work environment. Check out the Appendixes for more information.

I suggest getting friends in the civilian workforce to help you transform those military duties, responsibilities, and accomplishments into valuable intellectual property that will serve as an impressive calling card to hiring managers with open positions. Have friends ask questions about the nature of the duty, responsibility, and accomplishment; have them help you fill in the Task→Core Competency→Functional Expertise charts from this chapter; and talk about how it can all roll over into expertise that any hiring manager can easily understand and recognize.

Chapter 11
Postscript

OVER THE YEARS AS A HIRING MANAGER, I have taken notice of certain individuals I had a hand in hiring who went on to enjoy highly successful careers for themselves. These people more often than not showed personal and professional initiative, a willingness to learn, displayed a flexible attitude toward projects, had great people skills, demonstrated excellent communication abilities, and possessed an ability to navigate successfully through organizational structures (and the politics that go with them).

I have categorized these abilities into five major qualities that each of these individuals possessed:

- A sense of *project ownership*
- A sense of *project urgency*
- A sense of *personal integrity*
- A desire to *help others succeed*
- An attitude of *being "self-employed"*

A Sense of Project Ownership

A sense of project ownership is prized by hiring managers everywhere because it conveys that an individual brings to the table a quality mindset, a get-it-done-right-the-first-time approach to whatever project is being undertaken. An individual with this attitude shows concern for budgets, schedules, and meeting customer requirements—whether that customer is the job foreman, the CEO, or the consumer in the marketplace. It is a forward-moving focus that can not help but pull in others in its wake. People who display a sense of project ownership are not clock-watchers—they often "call it a day" at some logical stopping point in their task, not when the clock says 5pm or when the whistle blows (union rules not withstanding).

A Sense of Project Urgency

A sense of project urgency implies that an individual's approach to project work is immediate, purposeful, and resolute. Such determined individuals are decisive about which solution to a problem to embrace after a careful evaluation of the problem, the potential causes, and an assessment of all possible resolutions, and how those fixes should be implemented. Such folks rarely keep others waiting or guessing as to how to proceed next.

Personal Integrity

Personal integrity is a quality that, when tarnished, is hard to return to its original luster. And when it is lost altogether, is very difficult to recover. A person's integrity is wrapped up in their truthfulness about all matters, their honesty in dealing with people and projects, and their reliability to honor their word. Personal integrity is not a badge people wear on the outside, but it is more a reflection of the deeper nature of their character and moral, ethical fiber.

A Desire to Help Others Succeed

Many years ago early in my career, I heard some great advice from author and motivational speaker, Zig Ziglar: "If you help enough people get what they want, you'll eventually get what you want." That philosophy works best when it is a conscious heart-felt decision to help others *first* and not seen from the flip-side perspective: "To get what I want, I need to help others get what they want first." It is embracing a servant attitude that is so often lacking in the business world today. Imagine if Wall Street investment bankers, mortgage brokers, and auto company CEOs, and movers and shakers in Washington, D.C. had just made it their daily mantra: "how can I best serve your needs today?" we would not have 10-plus percent unemployment, record foreclosures, lost retirements, "gas guzzler" entitlement programs, and an economy struggling to find any sense of consistency.

One of the best displays of a servant attitude I have ever witnessed was from an administrative assistant name Amy. No matter what the complaint or who was complaining, Amy was first to offer an apology for any problems caused or inconveniences served up by others, which was usually followed up with "I will take care of that for you." When I overheard her defuse an incident with her kind words and smile, I took her aside and said "You have such an awesome servant attitude, and it's a pleasure to work with you." Her eyes immediately teared up and she replied, "That is the nicest thing anyone has said to me in the ten years I have worked here. You have just made it all worthwhile." Just a simple acknowledgement of someone's desire to help others first is usually all the reward such individuals accept, albeit grudgingly, because they do it without expectation of anything in return—it is an outward expression of their inner spirit.

In the same way a burning candle loses nothing to light another candle, so it is with helping others.

An Attitude of Being "Self-Employed"

Truly successful individuals always understand that no matter where the paycheck comes from, they really do work for themselves. Besides the skills, knowledge, and experience they bring to any job, project, or task, it is also the sense of project ownership, sense of project urgency, personal integrity, and helping others succeed that makes them "self-employed."

Contractors and consultants know what being self-employed is all about but sometimes people in hourly or salaried positions lose sight of the fact that they are self-employed as well. No one keeps anyone on the payroll out of the goodness of their hearts; it is the application of all those qualities mentioned in the previous paragraphs that keep the paychecks coming on a regular basis.

And what happens if you lose your job even though you have been working diligently to the best of your abilities? You were looking for a job when you found this last one, right? In the high-tech world and other fast-paced environments, job turnover is a common occurrence and folks accept it as a way of life. "Reductions in force" (RIFs, as HR calls them) happen for a variety of reasons, many of which are not tied to the overall economy.

One company I worked for had an unusual employee evaluation process. All employees in a particular job function were evaluated annually and their performances were forced under a normal distribution curve (the common bell-shaped curve seen in basic statistics textbooks). It did not matter if you had a department that consisted of all high-achieving individuals—managers had to force-fit only a few in the upper tail of the curve ("exceeded expectations"), stuff most of the remainder under the "bell" of the curve, and pack a few under the lower tail of the curve ("did not meet expectations"), meaning some type of "corrective action plan" was necessary to bring these workers up to accepted standard job performance within a three-month period; otherwise, they would lose their job. Managers had to defend their employee ratings with other managers as they competed for the money set aside for raises. If you had a non-assertive, meek manager who avoided confrontation, the raises were not going to be very good that year (a temporary setback as teams rarely had the same manager two years in a row, which presented a different set of problems).

No one looked forward to this stressful time of year, and many very good employees left the company for better positions elsewhere rather than face being subjected to this unfair performance evaluation. Most of the time, those folks went on to better paying jobs and more favorable working environments.

One division of a company I worked for was sold off to another engineering company. The vast majority of employees received offers of continued employment with this new company, but there were a handful of outstanding engineers who did not. Those who received offers of continued employment were puzzled initially why highly qualified co-workers were not extended offers of continued employment. Later, they discovered a common denominator was that at some time in the past, each of those engineers had a major disagreement with the division general manager over some aspect of an engineering project. All indications pointed to the conclusion that those incidents were factored in to whether they received offers of continued employment.

There is a happy ending. While some of those individuals had to endure a few jobless months (a generous severance package helped), six months later they were all working in higher paying positions at other companies, again proving the concept that no matter where your paycheck comes from, you will always be self-employed.

Many individuals developed these traits as they matured; some came in the door with them, having honed these abilities at other companies. The hard fact today is that even with such preferred individual qualities, there are no guarantees of jobs, let alone being called in for an interview.

However, taking the attitude of working for one's self provides several advantages. It insulates you against negative self-talk by reinforcing a positive you-are-in-control self-image. Rejection feels less and less about you personally and is really more about the economic and other factors controlling the job market. There is more empowerment in the feeling that "I work for ME" that propels you out the door or through the job websites each morning. That empowerment pushes you to become the unabashed self-promoter who has unique expertise that will be recognized by the right people, particularly if you know what challenges they are faced with, and how you can help them meet those issues head on.

A Final Word

If you are a *Star Trek* fan, you undoubtedly remember the *Kobayashi Maru* incident. Captain Kirk (no relation), as a young cadet at the Star Fleet Academy, became the only cadet to have successfully mastered the famous battle simulation, which presented a no-win scenario. The test forced cadets to make one of two choices: attempt to rescue the *Kobayashi Maru* that was under attack, and be destroyed in the process; or, leave it to be destroyed. Cadet Kirk secretly reprogrammed the battle simulation: he took a no-win situation created by a set of rules, and won by changing the rules. He went way outside the box.

You may have to change the rules of the game to be able to play better than anyone else, and that means doing more research, reading, networking, and taking some creative approaches to getting noticed (fresh-baked cookies and baseball tickets mentioned in the *Preface* were ways of "reprogramming" the existing scenario). It also means looking for opportunities where others only see problems. But most of all, you have to be persistent and not get caught up in the number of rejections you will receive for those positions to which you have applied.

Having once years ago spent more than nine months out of work and sent out more than 300 résumés over that same time period (and only one job interview), I do know the feeling for living for the mailman's arrival each day, or jumping when the phone rings, hoping it is an HR representative or hiring manager calling for a phone screen or to schedule an interview.

Salespeople know that for every "no" or door that is slammed in their face, they are one step closer to a "yes" and closing a sale. That persistent attitude sustains you during the "in-between" times of unemployment. For each "no" (or no response at all), you are one step closer to getting hired. You have to take it day by day, knowing you are in fact one day closer to being hired for that job you want.

No one addressed persistence better than the 30th President of the United States, Calvin Coolidge:

Nothing in this world can take the place of persistence. Talent will not; nothing is more common than unsuccessful people with talent. Genius will not; unrewarded genius is almost a proverb. Education will not; the world is full of educated derelicts. Persistence and determination alone are omnipotent. The slogan "press on" has solved and always will solve the problems of the human race.

These strategies, methodologies, and tactics have been proven over and over in companies where I have worked, and by many others who have followed them to land new jobs or change careers. They represent my experiences and observations in hiring manager positions that span a 20-year career, and as such, may differ from those of other hiring managers who have worked in different or even the same industries. I suppose I will know how different when they write their books. Nonetheless, I stand by the strategies, tactics, suggestions, and most of all the proof that these techniques have worked and continue to do so in any employment environment.

Please let me know the success you have had with the information in this book as I want to celebrate your good fortune with you. If you would like my assistance helping you put together your *PSKE Portfolio*, refer to the information in Appendix C, or contact me directly.

With that, I wish you all the very best in your job and career endeavors wherever that journey takes you.

Now let's get busy!

J.T. Kirk
jtkirk@jtkirk-author.com

Appendix A
Resources

BACK BEFORE THE DAYS of online search engines, many books contained resource lists in Appendixes. The information on those lists remained viable for longer than it does today because information traveled much slower before the Internet. Not so today; with information being transmitted at lightning speed and the ubiquity of desktop computers, laptop computers, and phones with Internet functionality, having a "Best of" or "Top 10" list in print in the back of a book does not make sense because any list is out of date as soon as the search engine results are displayed. Just think of how often the Amazon.com book rankings change throughout a single day.

Books on Cover Letters, Résumés, Interview Techniques, and Salary Negotiation

Use your favorite search engine to search on "Top 10 Books on <search term> "and you will have your list. The search engine method keeps the list fresh all the time rather than relying on a printed, and quickly out-of-date list here.

Avoid investing money in books with titles such as *600 Cover Letters for Every Job...* or *999 Résumés for Every Job Imaginable...* such books can only offer the most basic types of cover letters and résumés for the positions they address—and none of them will be close to describing your exact and unique skills, knowledge, and experience. You also do not want to be paying for a book that also shows you 998 other résumés that do not interest you. If your local public library carries such titles, by all means check them out and look through them.

Best Websites for Cover Letter, Resume, and Interview Advice

Like the book list, this list is a dynamic one and changes often. Enter as a search phrase "Top 10 websites for <enter term>". But here are ten job websites that offer quite a lot of great advice, tips, and strategies on the job front:

www.careerbuilder.com

www.monster.com

www.jobcentral.com

www.yahoo.com

www.collegerecruiter.com

www.jobfox.com

www.indeed.com

www.simplyhired.com

www.net-temps.com

www.hound.com

Best-Paid Contract Jobs

According to the *BusinessWeek* website, these are the best paying contracting jobs available. Details are available at **www.images.businessweek.com/ss/09/06/0630_contract_ workers**

Database Administrator (mean annual pay: $80,300; degree required)
Software Developer ($71,900; B.S. degree required)
IT Business Analyst ($68,500; B.S. degree required)
Software Development Test Engineer ($66,500; B.S. degree required)
Systems Administrator ($59,000; B.S. degree required)
IT Network Administrator ($57,100; A.S. degree required)
Physical Therapy Assistant ($53,500; A.S. degree required)
Occupational Therapy Assistant ($47,000; A.S. degree required)
Heavy Equipment Operator ($44,900; no degree required)
Information Technology Specialist ($43,500; B.S. degree required)
Graphics Artist/Designer ($43,300; B.S. degree required)
Computer/Network Support Technician ($43,200; B.S. degree required)
Truck Driver: Tractor-Trailer ($42,800; no degree required)

Official Military Service Documentation that may be Required by Potential Employers

The following documents summarize various segments of your military career (assignment history, promotions, security clearance, job performance, foreign languages, personal data):

- Army
  - o Officer Record Brief (ORB)
  - o Personnel Qualification Record (PQR)-enlisted
- Marines
  - o Office Qualification Records (OQR)

- o Enlisted Service Record Book (SRB)
- Navy
  - o Enlisted Service Record (ESR)
  - o Officer Service Record (OSR)
- Air Force
  - o NCO and Officer Personnel Brief

Report of Separation (DD-214)

This document contains information on your military job specialty, service dates, military training/education, decorations, medals, badges, citations, campaign awards, retirement benefits, and character of discharge. Replacements available from:

www.archives.gov/veterans/military-service-records/get-service-records.html

Verification of Military Experience and Training Document (VMAT)

This document itemizes your military experience and training that may be useful when preparing résumés, job applications, and other appropriate and related documents. This document can be used as proof you have met training or education requirements to qualify for civilian jobs, certifications, licenses, or other programs. Visit the VMET website to learn more at

www.dmdc.osd.mil/appj/vmet/index.jsp

Note: Access is limited to individuals who served actively after 10/1/90. Login is required.

Education and Job Training Resources

The American Institute for Full Employment is a nonprofit public policy research and development center. Their website contains a wealth of links to federal, state, and local government agencies that offer welfare and unemployment insurance information for job seekers. Check them out at:
www.fullemployment.org

National Association of Veterans Upward Bound Project
http://navub.org/

Veterans Upward Bound (VUB) is a free U.S. Department of Education program designed to help eligible U.S. military veterans refresh their academic skills so that they can successfully complete the postsecondary school of their choosing.

To be eligible for participation in a VUB program, an individual must be a low-income and/or first-generation college (meaning that neither of your parents have a four-year college degree) student, having served at least 180 days of active federal service, and have a discharge that is OTHER than dishonorable.

Currently, there are 46 VUB programs nationwide and in Puerto Rico and Guam ready to serve veterans.

Veterans Organizations, Associations, Websites with Job Info

Use a search engine to find more veterans websites with job information, but here is a starter list:

www.hireahero.org
www.hireheroesUSA.org
www.militaryhire.com
www.iraqwarveterans.org/military.htm
www.veteranstoday.com
www.militaryveteranjobs.com
www.taonline.com/veteranpages
www.recruitmilitary.com
www.welcomebackveterans.org/jobs
www.bushcares.org
www.helmetstohardhats.org
www.camppatriot.org
www.military.com
www.baseops.net

U.S. Department of Labor/Bureau of Labor Statistics

www.bls.gov
Employment Projections 2008-2018:
www.bls.gov/news.release/ecopro.nr0.htm

Office of Publications and Special Studies:
www.bls.gov/opub

Employment and Training Administration:
www.doleta.gov

Be sure to check out the many other great links on the USDOL/BS websites.

Appendix B
Cover Letter and Résumé Checklist

Cover Letters

- [ ] Addressed to a specific individual
- [ ] Use bulleted lists pulled from résumé
- [ ] Shows dollars saved/earned, costs avoided or percent efficiency improved (if that info is available)
- [ ] No longer than one page
- [ ] Contains more instances of "you/your" than "I/me"
- [ ] Tone shows awareness of hiring manager's issues; promotes "problem-solver profit center" attitude
- [ ] Demonstrates with evidence to support claims of "greatness" (**show** them, don't just **tell** them)
- [ ] Has a promotional tone that reinforces your skills, knowledge, experience—it's your brochure
- [ ] Close with promise to follow up in a few days and follow through with that promise
- [ ] Proofread carefully; run Spellchecker, and then have other people proofread it

Résumés

- [ ] Title block with name, phone number, email address
- [ ] Avoid email handles like sexygirl@yahoo.com or buffdude@hotmail.com—you want a job, right?
- [ ] Don't use your current work email address in your contact information—that should be obvious; get a free Gmail account from Google or Hot Mail account from Microsoft
- [ ] Place a professional message on your answering machine instead of that blast from *Nine Inch Nails* or *Van Halen* (unless you're expecting a call from a hiring manager in the music industry) just in case that call for an interview comes in when you're not home
- [ ] If you provide a URL to a website, ensure it presents you in the most favorable light possible because a hiring manager will look at it if you provide the link
- [ ] If you MUST put a link to a MySpace or Facebook page, be sure it represents you in a positive, professional manner; otherwise, don't link to it
- [ ] Don't include an "Objectives" section; instead, call it a "Professional Summary" or "Summary of Experience" and summarize, don't plead the obvious need for a job
- [ ] For reverse-chronological résumés, avoid using the phrase "responsible for..." because hiring managers want to know what you *did*, not what you were *supposed* to do.

☐ Use actions words (below) for accomplishments:

Acquired	Demonstrated	Oversaw
Administered	Formed	Performed
Audited	Hired	Planned
Calculated	Created	Improved
Reviewed	Changed	Implemented
Maintained	Taught	Coordinated
Managed	Tested	Designed
Published	Edited	Wrote
Supervised	Directed	Built

☐ Avoid narratives; use bulleted lists

☐ Avoid long paragraphs, use short sentences

☐ Supplemental information: use only if it pertains to the position for which you are interviewing

☐ Entry-level positions: one page résumé is enough

☐ Experienced people: one page per 10 years experience is sufficient; experience older than 10 years warrants only a one-line mention rather than bulleted list of accomplishments, responsibilities

☐ If you list "Debate Society" on your résumé but omit details, you may be asked: "What did you do with the Debate Society?" If you just attended meetings, it's natural for interviewers to doubt validity of other claims on the résumé; in other words—your supplemental information must show some involvement other than just being a name on a member roster

☐ Stick with typical familiar fonts: Times New Roman, Helvetica, Arial, Palatino, Georgia, Verdana are all good (use one style for headings; another for bullet lists and paragraphs) but try to keep it to only two font styles and no more than three different font sizes

☐ Go easy on bold and italic—sparing use only for emphasis

☐ White space is a design element; leave generous margins all the way around and between major information blocks to facilitate scanning of key information and for making notes in margins

☐ Use hierarchical order for your reverse-chronological résumé:

-Title block/Contact Information
-Professional Summary
-Experience (most recent first)
-Education
-Supplemental information

☐ Use a hierarchical order for your functional résumé:

-Title block/Contact Information

-Professional Summary

-Functional Areas of Expertise (begin with the most relevant to the position for which you are applying)

-Supplemental information (make it pertain to the position for which you are applying)

-Education

☐ Beware of any advice to make your résumé "a knockout marketing piece"; that's the job of your cover letter—to sell the sizzle; the résumé helps package you as the consummate professional in your field of expertise; make it look professional

☐ Scrub your links to "favorite music videos", "favorite YouTube videos", and blogs for the same reasons

☐ Don't include your photos, gender, age, sexual orientation, physical characteristics, or religion as those items can open the door to discrimination or automatic rejection based on those qualities rather than your skills, experience, and knowledge

☐ Maintain more than one version of your résumé to emphasize different expertise; don't try to cram it all on one résumé

☐ Write objectively in the third person

☐ List special education honors, awards, extracurricular activities if they are relevant

☐ Don't mention interests, hobbies, family, etc. They take up precious real estate on a résumé and just don't belong here; interviewers may ask you about them, but keep the details few (don't say you like "hunting"; instead say you enjoy "outdoor activities" or you like "hunting, fishing, and camping" which is less threatening to PETA members. Avoid indicating you enjoy participating in "wildlife population control" as a euphemism for "hunting" as one candidate told me during an interview)

☐ Most hiring managers expect candidates to have a list of references, so stating on your résumé "List of references available on request" may be unnecessary

☐ Save your documents as a Word .doc file (avoid the .docx format used in Microsoft Office 2007 Word) and PDF for ease of email attachment

☐ I've been called "old school" for my position on keeping résumés to one to two pages; some recruiters, résumé writers, and career coaches push for putting it all in an "appendix" that's part of the résumé—don't do it as it will be information overload—keep the publications list, patents list, artistic credits, awards, etc. as separate elements of your *PSKE Portfolio*—it will definitely work more in your favor (the "old school" method respects other people's time—which shows you understand it's about what *they* need to see, and not about *you* want to show them)

☐ Update your résumés (both kinds) every six to nine months

☐ Before you place anyone on your References list, be sure to clear it with them first, and alert them after you have an interview that a hiring manager or an HR representative may be contacting them

☐ Use only those individuals as references who can speak to your personal integrity, accomplishments, and professionalism and who are themselves articulate (don't try to use your gym buddy or frat brother to masquerade as one of your professional references)

☐ Don't include "reasons for leaving" your previous or current job on a résumé; you may be asked in an interview, so the only good responses are "workforce reduction" (if that's what happened) or "to pursue other opportunities that make better use of my expertise and provide more challenge"; if you were fired from your last job, don't lie about it—it can be easy to verify

☐ If you aren't writing articles for your profession or industry newsletters or journals, start now; a publications list conveys expertise, lending more credibility to the accomplishments on your résumé

☐ Proofread it, run Spellchecker on it, and have others proofread it, too—your eye sees what is supposed to be there on the page; others will see what is actually there

☐ Include only coursework that led to certification or licensing; list any pertinent training you've had that was at least 3 days long and offered by a recognized organization (such as the American Management Association, Society for Human Resource Management, Project Management Institute, etc.)

☐ Be careful about "stretching" your skills, knowledge, or expertise level in any area on your résumé as the interview team may design behavioral interviewing questions around what you claim to know or have accomplished

☐ Be able to discuss at length any and all bullet items and statements on your résumé, and be able to interject that information as necessary at any point in an interview (whether you initiate discussion on the topic or you use that information to respond to questions)

Appendix C
Free Online Cover Letter and Résumé Assessments

HOW DOES YOUR COVER LETTER and résumé stack up to what you've seen in this book? A quick, easy, and free way to find out is to visit www.jtkirk-author.com and run both your résumé and cover letter through the FREE online assessment programs. Just answer the questions, submit your responses, and you'll receive an email with the results—simple as that. You'll also get a link to FREE tip sheets for résumés, cover letters, job interviews, salary negotiation, job/career planning, and more.

Need More Help? Other Programs Available to Assist You with Cover Letter and Résumé Writing

Here are just a few other programs that may be of interest to you. Be sure to check out any and all programs that do the work for you and charge you money. Find out what their guarantee is if they are the ones creating cover letters and résumés.

Military.myresumemanager.com

$170: résumé rewrite

$249:

- Professional Military Conversion Résumé
- "Free" cover letter and "Free" thank-you letter
- "Free" web/ text formatting
- 100% money-back guarantee (because they do the work)

www.resume.info/military-resume-writing

$249: Same as above plus

- 3 "free" ebooks;
- 100% money-back guarantee (because they do the work)

While there are many other programs available to you, I believe mine offer the best value available when you consider what you get for your money, because it's a collaboration that also teaches you how to prepare your own PSKE Portfolios for the years and career that lie ahead of you.

Confessions of a Hiring Manager
Personal Consultations with J.T. Kirk

If you are continuing to struggle with defining your job or career strategy, or need my personal assistance with developing the necessary documentation for your own *PSKE Portfolio* to move forward, send me an email (jtkirk@jtkirk-author.com) or visit my website at www.jtkirk-author.com for more details.

To be clear, I am not offering nor can I offer a guarantee that you will find a job with my personal assistance as there are other variables beyond any one person's control (including mine) such as changes in hiring practices, job market fluctuations at different times and in different regions of the country, and the overall up and down gyrations of the economy. In fact, beware of anyone making *any* kind of guarantees of finding you a job or career and requiring an upfront payment. The only guarantee that can be offered *realistically* with such services, such as a résumé writing service, is that you are satisfied that the résumé *someone else wrote* adequately reflects your skills, knowledge, and experience.

However, my personal assistance will help you leverage your skills, knowledge, and experience to their fullest to maximize your chances of getting noticed by hiring managers, increase the probability of getting an interview, and secure an excellent overall compensation package that helps support your specific personal situation in the shortest time possible.

I offer two different programs to fit your specific needs and budget: a one-hour phone consultation and the *Professional Collaboration Package*. Each step includes an over-the-phone question-and-answer session before moving forward.

Through August 31, 2010, I am offering readers of *Confessions of a Hiring Manager* discounted fees for my personal assistance. The one-hour phone consultation is $179 (a savings of $75 off the normal fee of $250). The *Professional Collaboration Package* is available for $375 (a savings of $124 off the normal fee of $499). Here's what the package includes:

- Review/written assessment of your career objectives
- Review/written analysis of your current résumé
- Review/written analysis of two résumé drafts (one reverse chronological and one functional or two reverse chronological or two functional versions)
- Review/written analysis of two cover letter drafts
- One 30-minute interview coaching session over the phone
- One 30-minute salary package negotiation coaching session over the phone
- Vinyl portfolio to hold your *PSKE Portfolio* documents and leave-behinds
- You do the work with my guidance, coaching, suggestions
- There is no charge for an initial 20-minute phone consultation

Confessions **of a Hiring Manager**
Keynote Speaking, Workshops

Does your organization, corporation, or association need a keynote speaker or full-day hands-on workshop that has attendees designing and creating the elements of a *PSKE Portfolio* (cover letters, résumé, support documentation), learning how to control job interviews, and negotiating the best possible compensation package? Please have the appropriate person contact me at jtkirk@jtkirk-author.com for a complete information kit.

CONFESSIONS OF A HIRING MANAGER

Book and Special Report Order Form

Confessions of a Hiring Manager (available March 30, 2010)	$19.95
Confessions of a Hiring Manager Workbook (available April 30, 2010)	$10.00
Special Report No. 1: Creating a Résumé that Gets a Hiring Manager's Attention	$5.00
Special Report No. 2: Cover Letters: Selling the Sizzle of Your Expertise	$5.00
Special Report No. 3: Just for Veterans: Transitioning Military Skills, Knowledge, and Experience to the Civilian Job Market	$5.00
Special Report No. 4: Getting the Job: Controlling the Job Interview	$5.00
Special Report No. 5: Negotiating the Best Job Offer	$5.00
Special Report No. 6: Planning Your Career or Job Strategy	$5.00
One-Hour Phone Consultation (through August 31, 2010 only-rate returns to $250 after August 31)	$179.00
Professional Collaboration Package (through August 31, 2010 only-rate returns to $499.00 after August 31)	$375.00

Texas residents add 8% sales tax on books/Special Reports

Postage/handling: ($2.75 for first book, $1.00 each additional)

TOTAL ENCLOSED

Mail orders:
Kings Crown Publishing
6705 Highway 290 West, Suite 502-247
Austin, TX 78735

Online orders:
www.jtkirk-author.com and www.kingscrownpublishing.com

KINGS
CROWN
PUBLISHING

Visit **www.kingscrownpublishing.com** for more upcoming projects.

Anatomy of a Winning Book Proposal by Donn LeVie, Jr.

So how does a unique idea for a book project from a relatively unknown author get the enthusiastic buy-in and participation from 35 of the world's best classical guitarists? Author Donn LeVie, Jr. details how he came up with the idea for the book project, how he "sold" the idea to the world's top classical guitar performers to provide essays for the project, and how he got worldwide distribution of this project "first" for the classical music world. How do you compensate 35 essay contributors and still make money in such a project? You discard the old, tired, publishing paradigm and all its assumptions, and propose a sensible approach where everyone involved in the project enjoys the financial reward.

Christmas 2010 release. $19.95

Don't forget the *Confessions of a Hiring Manager Workbook!* Available April 30, 2010.

It's All About HYMN: Essays on Reclaiming Sacred and Traditional Music for Worship by Donn LeVie, Jr.

Classical guitarist, church musician, and author Donn LeVie, Jr. invites music leaders, congregations, and church musicians to honestly assess how well their worship music uplifts the gospel. Here, they will discover there is no room for personal preference where spiritual discernment, established church music criteria, and scriptural guidance must give wing to our voices in praise and adoration of an Almighty God.

288 pages, $16.99 retail (**September 2008**)

50 Things You Can Do NOW to Keep Your Job by J.T. Kirk

Veteran hiring manager J.T. Kirk reveals 50 things you can do to help keep your job today. Author of *Confessions of a Hiring Manager,* J.T. Kirk strikes again with *50 Things You Can Do NOW to Keep Your Job.* Kirk gives you his insight on what skills, knowledge, and personality characteristics managers value when they have to choose between "keepers" and those destined for workforce reduction. It's not always the smartest person who makes the cut, and Kirk tells you why in this no-holds-barred book.

Christmas 2010 release. $19.95

For a Higher Purpose: The Significance and Meaning of Sacred Music for Worship by Donn LeVie, Jr.

Classical guitarist, church musician, and author Donn LeVie, Jr. follows up the popular *It's All About HYMN: Essays on Reclaiming Sacred and Traditional Music for Worship* with more scripturally derived guidance for selecting music for worship. *For a Higher Purpose* contains success stories, interviews, and insight from music directors, choir directors, congregations, and church musicians on how they were able to move away from entertainment-style worship music to choices that uplift the Gospel and in a manner befitting a loving God.

2011 release. $19.95

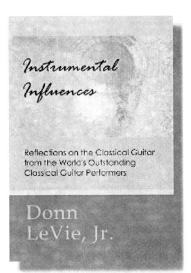

Instrumental Influences: Reflections on the Classical Guitar from the World's Outstanding Classical Guitar Performers by Donn LeVie, Jr.

Over the centuries, the classical guitar in its various forms has inspired musicians and composers to create some of the world's most beautiful music. The elements of mastering the classical guitar have parallels in other areas of life; some parallels are more obvious than others, while others reveal themselves over time. Now, in the words of 30 of the world's outstanding classical guitar performers, they relate how the lessons of performance, of study, and of practice relate to other areas of life.

Christmas 2010 release. $19.95

Kings Crown Publishing Book Order Form

Confessions of a Hiring Manager (available 3/30/ 2010) $19.95

Confessions of a Hiring Manager Workbook (available 4/30/ 2010)
$10.00

*It's All About HYMN: Essays on Reclaiming Sacred and
Traditional Music for Worship* (Donn LeVie, Jr.) $16.99
(September 2008)

50 Things You Can Do NOW to Keep Your Job (J.T. Kirk)
(Available for Christmas 2010) $19.95

*Instrumental Influences: Reflections on the Classical Guitar
from the World's Outstanding Classical Guitar Performers*
(Donn LeVie, Jr.) (Available 11/1/2010)
                                                                                      $19.95
Anatomy of a Winning Book Proposal (Donn LeVie, Jr.)
(Available Christmas 2010)

**For a Higher Purpose: The Significance and Meaning of Sacred
Music for Worship** (Donn LeVie, Jr.) (Available 2011) $19.95

Texas residents add 8% sales tax on books/Special Reports

Postage/handling: ($2.75 for first book, $1.00 each additional)

                                        TOTAL ENCLOSED:

Mail orders:

Kings Crown Publishing
6705 Highway 290 West
Suite 502-247
Austin, TX 78735

Online orders:
www.kingscrownpublishing.com

All prices subject to change. Check publisher website for prices/availability.

LaVergne, TN USA
27 April 2010
180720LV00001B/3/P